TINY HOUSE COOKING

175+ RECIPES
Designed to Create
BIG FLAVOR
in a Small Space

D1275217

Foreword by Ryan Mitchell
Author of *Tiny Houses Built with Recycled Materials*

Adams Media
New York   London   Toronto   Sydney   New Delhi

Adams Media
An Imprint of Simon & Schuster, Inc.
57 Littlefield Street
Avon, Massachusetts 02322

First Adams Media trade paperback edition May 2018

ADAMS MEDIA and colophon are trademarks of Simon & Schuster.

For information about special discounts for bulk purchases, please contact Simon & Schuster Special Sales at 1-866-506-1949 or business@simonandschuster.com.

The Simon & Schuster Speakers Bureau can bring authors to your live event. For more information or to book an event contact the Simon & Schuster Speakers Bureau at 1-866-248-3049 or visit our website at www.simonspeakers.com.

Interior design by Heather McKiel
Photographs by James Stefiuk

Manufactured in the United States of America

10 9 8 7 6 5 4 3 2 1

Library of Congress Cataloging-in-Publication Data
Adams Media, firm.
Tiny house cooking.
Avon, Massachusetts: Adams Media, 2018.
Includes index.
LCCN 2017055515 (print) | LCCN 2017060448 (ebook) | ISBN 9781507207147 (pb) |
ISBN 9781507207154 (ebook)
LCSH: Cooking for two. | Canned foods. | LCGFT: Cookbooks.
LCC TX714 (ebook) | LCC TX714 .T566 2018 (print) | DDC 641.5/612--dc23
LC record available at https://lccn.loc.gov/2017055515

ISBN 978-1-5072-0714-7
ISBN 978-1-5072-0715-4 (ebook)

Contains material adapted from the following titles published by Adams Media, an Imprint of Simon & Schuster, Inc.: *The Everything® Cooking for Two Cookbook* by David Poran, copyright © 2005, ISBN 978-1-59337-370-2; *The Everything® Quick and Easy 30-Minute, 5-Ingredient Cookbook* by Linda Larsen, copyright © 2006, ISBN 978-1-59337-692-5; *The Everything® Vegetarian Cookbook* by Jay Weinstein, copyright © 2002, ISBN 978-1-58062-640-8; *The Everything® Stir-Fry Cookbook, 2nd Edition* by Nam Nguyen, copyright © 2013, ISBN 978-1-4405-6157-3; and *The Everything® Easy Mediterranean Cookbook* by Peter Minaki, copyright © 2015, ISBN 978-1-4405-9240-9.

CONTENTS

FOREWORD

Tiny homes have inspired people across the globe to make a huge change and live smaller. As more and more people turn to this way of life, they need practical advice on every aspect of tiny living. While tiny living has many advantages, it is not without its challenges. The biggest challenge is how to pack your rich and complex life into a small space. Tiny homes often range from 150 to 400 square feet for a single person or couple—dramatically smaller than today's average home of 2,600 square feet. So it makes sense that in such small spaces you tend to take a closer look at how you live your life.

In *Tiny House Cooking* you will learn how to meet your needs when it comes to cooking delicious meals for yourself, your family, and your friends in a small space. Just because you have a small space to prepare your meals doesn't mean you have to sacrifice cooking delicious meals. In tiny homes you learn to maximize the space you have, and this couldn't be truer than in the kitchen. In an age where there is a kitchen gadget for just about every task, this book talks about getting back to the basics of cooking and life.

Cooking food is an essential part of daily life. Because of this fact, you need to think critically about how you can meet this need effectively in as small a space as possible. In a tiny house, square footage is at a premium and you must consider how you allocate it very carefully.

Tiny living is a life of intention and deliberate choices. You are choosing to build the right life for you. You have taken a step back to consider every aspect of your life and decided on an alternative course so you can build the life you want to live—one where you are empowered to live, work, and spend your free time as you see fit.

In planning your journey to tiny living, you must consider many facets of your new life, including how you cook a simple and delicious meal, and this book will show you the most efficient and easy ways to do it.

—Ryan Mitchell

INTRODUCTION

If you live in a tiny house or are thinking of buying one, then you know that a tiny house provides everything you need to use less, save money, and simplify life down to the things that truly matter. But while tiny house living is replete with benefits, it is not without its challenges—one of which is the kitchen.

Many people have concerns about cooking in a tiny kitchen, but the reality is, with proper preparation and planning, you can cook meals that are fun and easy to make for you, your partner, and even guests! *Tiny House Cooking* provides you with more than 175 recipes that can all be cooked in a small-scale kitchen. These recipes are specifically designed with tiny house living in mind. For example:

- The recipes are made to serve two people so you won't have waste or hard-to-store leftovers. (Plus, you can easy double the recipes if you are having guests.)
- All the recipes are designed to be cooked on a two-burner cooktop so there is no need for other appliances, like ovens, toaster ovens, or microwaves, that often take up valuable space in your kitchen.
- The recipes use very few pots and pans because in a tiny house you need to make the most of your kitchen space!
- These recipes use only fresh and canned foods because freezer space is often at a minimum.

With these items in mind, in this book you'll find tasty recipes for every meal, including Creamy Goat Cheese Scramble, Smoked Turkey and Wild Rice Soup, Curry and Coconut Steamed Mussels, Cuban Pork Chops, and even desserts like No-Bake Apple Cookies, and Chocolate Raspberry Pie.

You don't have to sacrifice when it comes to cooking in your tiny house kitchen; in fact, there is no need for your mealtimes to change dramatically at all. With a little forethought and some careful prep, you'll be enjoying delicious and satisfying meals from your kitchen, no matter what its size!

CHAPTER 1

Cooking in a Tiny House

Downsizing is a growing trend that has led numerous people to turn to smaller spaces. Many people are opting to move into tiny houses for a simpler life, but others downsize to smaller homes and compact apartments as well. Yet just because people are choosing to live smaller, it doesn't mean they don't still need to cook a delicious and wholesome meal.

Cooking in a Small Space

Tiny houses are often 400 square feet or smaller for singles or couples. People are making this shift to smaller living for many reasons, such as to get out of debt, to live better lives, to retire earlier, and to spend more time with family and friends. Tiny living is focused on building quality lives with the ones who matter to you.

When you consider what a home is, you find that it is a structure that provides several functions for you to live your life. One of these is having a place to prepare and sit down for a meal. Even though you have only limited space, you will need to allocate a fair bit of it to this task. When thinking about how large or small a kitchen should be in your tiny house, take the following into account:

- How often do you actually cook meals at home now?
- How much do you enjoy cooking?
- What are your favorite things to cook, and how does that help inspire what will be in your kitchen?
- What tasks can be performed by multi-function items versus those with a single purpose?

When considering these questions, be honest with yourself. How much do you actually cook? If you're a person who loves to dine out at restaurants the majority of the time, a very basic kitchenette might be right for you. If you're a serious home cook who loves to cook and spend time in the kitchen, you might want to dedicate a bit more space to cooking.

The best indicator of how much you'll actually use your tiny house's kitchen is how often you use your current kitchen. Make your kitchen just big enough to suit your current needs because past behavior is the strongest indicator of future behavior. The beauty of tiny homes is that you're able to design and build a space that is right for you and your particular way of living.

In the end your kitchen and home need to be as unique as you are. Deciding what is right for you is critical to making your house a home—a place where you are comfortable, can enjoy your time, and can have a great meal with friends and family.

Think about Your Kitchen Plan

An important step when considering the design of your kitchen, as well as the rest of the house, is to break down exactly what you do in your own kitchen. You need a space to store shelf-stable goods, a fridge to keep things cold, a countertop to prepare food, a stove to heat things, a block to chop up food, and a sink to wash dishes.

Take a moment to sit down and think through a typical meal and how you cook it. Make a list of the things that you do in your current kitchen and how often you do them. Using this list, you can make a more informed decision on the placement and size of each item.

Another popular kitchen design principle is the kitchen work triangle, three points that are made up by the sink, the fridge, and the stove. If you imagine these three points making up a triangle, you ideally want them to be close to each other with nothing obstructing the flow between them to make your prepping, cooking,

and cleaning easy. Consider the placement and flow between these three points.

Refrigeration

When it comes to fridges you should go with 4 cubic feet per person; if you're really into cooking or someone who likes to cook from fresh every time, consider 5–6 cubic feet per person. If you are considering a mini fridge size, it's best to have a mini fridge and a separate unit for a freezer, as the combination units tend to freeze poorly. It's also worth considering mounting the mini fridge off the ground where you can more easily see into it without stooping.

Washing Food and Dishes

The sink is one of the key corners of the triangle and often is the focus of the start of prep and the end of a meal with cleaning dishes. Everyone has their opinions on sinks, but you should not be afraid to splurge on your sink and faucet. They can be expensive, but it's one of the things that you'll be using multiple times a day, so it's good to get one you love. If you end up going with a shallower countertop, consider a single-hole faucet that you can mount to the side. That way your basin can take advantage of the full countertop depth.

Food Preparation

The French have a phrase, *mise en place*, which translates to "everything in its place." It's the notion that you should prep all your ingredients, portion them out, dice/chop, and lay out everything before you start cooking. In addition to making you a more efficient cook, it's also a key concept to successfully cook in a tiny house. When you're cooking on a small cooktop and have limited counter space, if you are trying to prep and cook at the same time, it can get very cumbersome. You should take the time to prep everything ahead of time and then fully clear off the countertops before you start cooking. Consider how you'll go about cooking in your future tiny house: what the workflow will look like, and what steps you'll take in cooking your favorite dishes.

Cooking

Realize that living in a small space may lead you to consider different ways of cooking your food. For example, you may cook whole meals on your grill outside, cook a roast in a solar oven on a hot sunny day, or use a portable butane stovetop outside on a folding table if a dish is particularly fragrant (smells can fill up a tiny house fast, and you may not want odors to be trapped in your small space).

Stovetop

Living tiny means you'll have to adapt to cooking on a smaller cooktop. For most people a two-burner stovetop is the sweet spot and will meet the needs of nearly all of your daily cooking. You can still cook more complex and fancier dishes, but it isn't every day that you will cook a four-course meal. You should choose your cooktop for your everyday needs, not the special occasion dishes that you may only cook a few times a year. A two-burner stove offers the perfect balance between space and functionality. For this reason, all the recipes you'll find in this book are meant to be prepared on a two-burner stovetop. You will be amazed at the decadent and delicious meals you can prepare in this small arena.

Baking

While none of the recipes in this book requires an oven or toaster oven, baking in these appliances is certainly worth discussing. Many compact options for baking often fall short of most people's needs to bake a good loaf of bread or properly roast meats and vegetables. If you just want to bake a batch of brownies or cookies, you'll most likely be fine, but make sure you spend some time doing your research on the oven that you choose. Many tiny house owners opt to forgo a traditional oven and buy a quality countertop toaster oven. You could also supplement your baking outside the home by building a wood-fired pizza oven (perhaps on a patio), which allows you to get higher temperatures and a more even heat for better baking or roasting.

Other Kitchen Concerns

In addition to the three points of your kitchen triangle there are a few other kitchen options you'll need to consider, such as where to store your food, how to pare down your appliances, and what to to with your food waste and trash.

Countertop Appliances and Utensils

In the kitchen there are a million appliances, gadgets, and utensils that you can buy to make things just a little bit easier. In a tiny house you should focus on the absolute basics. Most great cooks rely on a very basic set of tools to do most of their work. Here is a general list to get you started:

- Skillet (with lid if possible)
- Saucepan

- Stockpot (or large pot for soups/stews)
- 2 sets silverware
- 2 bowls/plates
- 2 coffee mugs
- Can opener
- Whisk
- Mixing/salad bowl
- Colander
- 1–2 good knives
- Spatula
- Grater
- 2 cutting boards (1 for meat, 1 for everything else)
- Coffee pot/French press/tea pot
- 1 multipurpose measuring cup
- Some type of reusable leftover containers

It can be easy to have a tool for everything, but you should start to pare down your kitchen now, before you even move into a tiny house. You don't have to get rid of everything, but consider minimizing down to a more basic set and then putting everything else in a box in the closet.

With this approach you can find your own ideal set of implements for what you really need while eliminating the clutter. From there you can design your kitchen to hold exactly what you need and nothing more.

Pantry

Part of any kitchen is a place to store your dry goods and shelf-stable items. It can be hard to figure out where to tuck these items, but you should look at what you store now and design cabinets around that. You'll find it's more convenient to standardize containers for dry goods to maximize your space; for example, after shopping place things like flour, pasta, oatmeal, rice, and cereal into containers that all stack well. This eliminates the awkwardness of varied packaging sizes and shapes. You can also design your shelves around the standardized containers so that everything fits and you maximize the space. Having similar containers also looks more presentable and reduces the feeling of clutter when everything is neatly uniform on the shelf or in a cabinet.

Handling Trash and Recycling

A commonly forgotten item when planning a small kitchen is where you are going to keep your various bins for kitchen waste. Food packaging is often the number one source of trash in a tiny home. When at all possible you'll want to consider sourcing food items without packaging (bulk food stores); where you can't avoid it, you can opt for packaging that can be composted or recycled.

Trash

Dealing with trash is an unavoidable component of modern life, no matter the size of your house, but you can take some very simple steps to reduce how much trash you create. It's easy to fall into the mental trap of thinking that if you recycle most things then you are doing okay, but in reality it starts before that. It all starts at the source: where you buy things.

Your first impulse should be to actively refuse to create trash to begin with. You can do this by:

- Considering where you do your shopping. For example, go to the farmers' market, where they don't overpackage food, instead of a big chain grocery store that packages everything in layers of foam and plastic.

- Asking for or bringing a reusable mug to the coffee shop.
- Shopping at bulk food stores, where you can bring your own storage bags.

Taking the time to think critically about the simple things you can do during your daily purchases can have a big impact and make living in a smaller space easier. The less you bring into your home to begin with, the less you have to store, process, or occupy your trash bin.

In terms of your tiny house, it is important that you don't forget to designate a place, or build in a space, to house your trash and recycling bins. People often forget this when planning out small kitchens, and then the trash bin seems like an afterthought, just dropped in a random place. If possible, build a pullout trash drawer into your kitchen so you can hide it out of sight.

Composting

It's inevitable that you will accumulate some trash even when trying to avoid it; you shouldn't be too hard on yourself when this happens. When you aren't able to avoid waste and it can't be reused or upcycled, it is better to keep the impact of it localized.

Composting is a great way to process some of the waste that is biodegradable. In most cases paper, cardboard, vegetable and fruit peelings, eggshells, and more can all be easily composted on-site. Not only will you produce great soil for your garden, but you also will remove mass from the waste stream and mitigate the resources used in the transport and processing of that trash.

For those who live where large compost piles might not be practical, the best composting setup is a simple plastic bin outside filled with red wiggler worms—vermicomposting. Essentially, it's composting that utilizes lots of worms to speed up the process of breaking down the material. Vermicomposting is forgiving to beginners and has the ability to process large amounts of food waste very quickly. In the end, you'll have some of the best potting soil you could ever hope for and you won't be adding to the waste stream.

Recycling

One of the ways you should shift your thinking when it comes to recycling is to view it as subsidiary to trash prevention. If you are recycling, it means you weren't able to prevent the trash or deal with it yourself in a proper manner. Every city or town has different capabilities for recycling, so check with your local municipality about what can and cannot be recycled.

Also, getting a recycling bin that is bigger than your trash bin reinforces your priority to recycle over just trashing something. Having a smaller trash bin can serve as an active reminder that if you have to keep emptying it again and again, you need to do a better job at preventing trash.

CHAPTER 2

Breakfast and Brunch

"LOST BREAD"

INGREDIENTS

Serves 2

---

2 thick slices crusty bread, about 2" thick

2 cups whole milk

8 large eggs, beaten

⅛ teaspoon salt

3 tablespoons butter

1. Allow the bread to sit out uncovered 24–36 hours to go completely stale. Once bread is ready, place in a small dish just wide and deep enough to hold slices.
2. In a large bowl, mix together the milk, eggs, and salt and pour over the bread. Cover with plastic wrap and place a small dish on the top to prevent the bread from floating. Refrigerate overnight.
3. The next day, heat the butter in a medium skillet over medium heat. Remove the bread from the dish, add it to the skillet, and cook until very brown on all sides and no liquid escapes when the bread is squeezed, about 5 minutes per side. Serve warm.

FRENCH TOAST STUFFED WITH CREAM CHEESE AND JAM

INGREDIENTS

Serves 2

---

4 large eggs, beaten

1 cup whole milk

4 slices white bread

2 tablespoons butter, or as needed

3 tablespoons cream cheese

3 tablespoons jam of your choice

1. In a large bowl, mix together the eggs and milk. Soak the bread in the mixture 1 minute.
2. In a medium skillet over medium heat, melt the butter. Add the bread and fry well on both sides until golden brown, about 3–4 minutes per side.
3. Spread one side of 2 slices of the bread with the cream cheese. Top the slices with the jam and the remaining slices of bread. No syrup needed here.

 BUTTER IS BETTER

Butter has superior flavor over oil in many applications, especially breakfast cookery. It is the milk solids in the butter that brown when the butter is cooked and give up that rich and nutty flavor that only butter has. If you are going to be cooking over very high heat, butter is not recommended because it burns easily.

SOUR CREAM PANCAKES

INGREDIENTS

Serves 2

---

1 cup sour cream

2 large eggs

¼ cup all-purpose flour

2 teaspoons granulated sugar

⅛ teaspoon salt

Butter, as needed

1. In a medium bowl, mix together all the ingredients except the butter and let rest 10 minutes.
2. Lightly coat a medium nonstick pan with the butter. Pour about ¼ cup batter into the pan and cook over medium heat about 1 minute or until the surface is peppered with small bubbles. Flip very gently and cook about 1 more minute until nicely browned. Repeat with the remaining batter. Serve hot.

OATMEAL, BUTTERMILK, AND BANANA PANCAKES

INGREDIENTS

Serves 2

¼ cup instant oatmeal

½ cup buttermilk

1 large egg, beaten

2 tablespoons butter, plus more for pan, divided

¼ cup all-purpose flour

2 teaspoons granulated sugar

½ teaspoon baking powder

1 medium banana, sliced

1. In a medium bowl, mix together the oatmeal and the buttermilk and let stand 1 hour.
2. Add the egg, 1 tablespoon melted butter, flour, sugar, and baking powder. Let stand 10 minutes.
3. In a small skillet over medium-high heat, sauté banana slices in 1 tablespoon butter 1 minute. Set aside and keep warm.
4. Coat a nonstick pan with butter and heat over medium heat. Pour ¼ cup batter into the pan. Cook until the surface is evenly peppered with bubbles, about 2 minutes. Flip over and cook another 2 minutes. Repeat with the remaining batter. Serve with the bananas on top.

 COOKED BANANAS

Cooking bananas is a simple and effective way to change their flavor and texture. Bananas can be sautéed, fried in batter, broiled with sugar, grilled on a hot grill, and even boiled in their skins. Sugar, liqueur, and any number of flavorings can be added. Some cultures even eat cooked bananas in a savory manner by adding garlic or curry.

MAPLE-APPLE-BRANDY-CRANBERRY SAUCE

INGREDIENTS

Serves 2

2 tablespoons butter

1 large Granny Smith apple, peeled, cored, and sliced

2 tablespoons dried cranberries

¼ cup brandy

1 cup pure maple syrup

1. Melt the butter in a medium skillet over medium heat. Add the apples and sauté until golden brown and softened, about 5–8 minutes.
2. Add remaining ingredients, reduce heat to low, and cook 5 minutes. Keep warm and serve.

COOKING WITH ALCOHOL
When alcohol boils, 99 percent of the alcohol burns off. There are very small traces that remain, and this is important to know for people who have allergies. Always be cautious when adding alcohol to a hot pan, as it may burst into flames and cause some damage to either you or your kitchen.

PERFECT POACHED EGGS

INGREDIENTS

Serves 2

2 quarts water

1 tablespoon white vinegar

⅛ teaspoon salt

4 large eggs

1. Place the water in a medium pot. Bring the water to just under a boil and add the vinegar and salt.
2. Swirl the water in the pot with a large spoon very rapidly to form a fast-moving whirlpool. Crack each egg into a small bowl and drop in one at a time in the center of the whirlpool. Do not allow the water to boil. Cook 3 minutes for medium-soft yolks. Remove eggs from the water with a slotted spoon and drain on paper towels. Serve hot.

POACHING IN ADVANCE
You can pre-poach eggs in anticipation of a large group of people. Simply follow the directions in this recipe, and when the eggs are almost done, place them in a bath of ice water. This will stop the eggs from cooking. You can store the eggs in the cold water in the fridge up to 24 hours. When you are ready to serve them, simply drop them into hot water for about 30 seconds to reheat.

PEANUT BUTTER AND CHOCOLATE PANCAKES

INGREDIENTS
Serves 2

½ cup sifted all-purpose flour

1 teaspoon baking powder

⅛ teaspoon salt

1 large egg

½ cup milk

1 tablespoon creamy peanut
    butter

1 teaspoon melted butter

1½ teaspoons butter

½ cup chocolate chips

1. In a large bowl, mix together the flour, baking powder, and salt.
2. In a small bowl, beat the egg. Add the milk and combine. Combine this with the flour mixture in the large bowl.
3. In a separate small bowl, add peanut butter and melted butter and mix well. Add to the batter.
4. Melt 1½ teaspoons butter in a medium nonstick pan or griddle over medium heat. Pour ¼ cup batter into the pan. Cook until small bubbles form on the surface of the pancake, about 2 minutes. Sprinkle the chocolate chips over the top, then flip the pancake and cook until golden brown. Repeat with the remaining batter.

CREAMY GOAT CHEESE SCRAMBLE

INGREDIENTS
Serves 2

2 tablespoons butter

6 large eggs

4 ounces soft fresh goat cheese

2 tablespoons minced fresh
    chives

⅛ teaspoon salt

⅛ teaspoon freshly ground
    black pepper

1. Melt the butter in a medium skillet over medium heat.
2. In a medium bowl, mix together the remaining ingredients well. Add to the warm butter and cook while constantly stirring to make the smallest curds possible. Stop cooking the eggs when they are still very moist, but not watery. Serve in warm bowls and eat with a spoon.

 EGGS AND SALMONELLA

It is true that undercooked eggs can carry salmonella. The bacteria are commonly found on the outside of the shell, and a careful washing may prevent transmission. The other way to prevent infection is to always cook eggs to at least 165°F. The problem with this is that it eliminates all sunny-side, over easy, poached, and soft-scrambled eggs. Buy eggs from refrigerated cases and in stores that do a brisk business and have lots of turnover of products on the shelf.

CHORIZO AND EGGS IN TORTILLAS

INGREDIENTS
Serves 2

4 ounces chorizo, minced

6 large eggs, beaten

⅛ teaspoon salt

⅛ teaspoon freshly ground
black pepper

4 (6") flour tortillas

1. Place the chorizo in a small skillet over medium heat and allow the fat to slowly render and the sausage to become crispy, about 4 minutes.
2. Add the eggs and cook as you would scrambled eggs. Season with salt and pepper and keep warm.
3. Warm the tortillas by holding them over a hot burner for a few seconds per side. Roll up the egg/chorizo mixture in the tortillas and eat like a taco.

 DIFFERENCES IN TORTILLAS

The basic types of tortillas are flour and corn. Most Americans are familiar with the crispy fried yellow corn tortillas used for hard tacos. However, in Mexico the soft white corn tortillas are much more popular. Flour tortillas are used more for wrapping burritos and soft tacos. Experiment with different tortillas and find your favorite.

SMOKED SALMON AND AVOCADO ON TOAST

INGREDIENTS
Serves 2

½ medium ripe avocado,
smashed

4 slices multigrain bread,
toasted

¼ teaspoon salt

¼ teaspoon freshly ground
black pepper

¼ cup minced red onion

1 medium ripe tomato, sliced

6 ounces smoked salmon

1. Spread avocado on 2 slices of the bread. Season with salt and pepper and top each with minced onion.
2. Top each slice with the tomato slices and salmon and then remaining bread. Serve immediately.

 HEALTHY FAT

Avocados are loaded with healthy fat. The type of fat found in avocados is also found in olive oil and walnuts. It is important to have fat in your diet, but make sure to vary the sources of these fats and not get them all from animal products, which are typically saturated fats. Saturated fats are unhealthier than most plant-based fats.

PASTRAMI HASH

INGREDIENTS

Serves 2

---

4 tablespoons butter, divided
½ pound pastrami, finely chopped
½ cup finely diced white onion
½ cup finely diced green bell pepper
1 large baked potato, skin on, chopped into marble-sized pieces
1 teaspoon Worcestershire sauce
⅛ teaspoon salt
⅛ teaspoon freshly ground black pepper

1. Heat 2 tablespoons butter in a heavy medium pan over medium heat until it stops bubbling. Add the pastrami, onion, and bell pepper and cook about 5 minutes.
2. Add the potato pieces, Worcestershire sauce, and the remaining butter to the pan. Mix well. Cook about 5 minutes per side or until very well crisped on each side. Season with salt and pepper and serve hot.

WHY IS IT CALLED "HASH"?

The term *hash* seems to come from the French *hachet*, which means "to cut into small pieces." There are many different types of hash, including the classics corned beef and roast beef. You can use almost any leftover meats to make a hash, and some fish, especially smoked fish, make wonderful hashes.

GRANOLA AND YOGURT PARFAIT

INGREDIENTS

Serves 2

---

2 cups plain low-fat yogurt
2 cups low-fat granola
1 pint strawberries, sliced

In a tall, clear glass, alternate layers of yogurt, granola, and berries until the glass is full. Make the top layer berries for an attractive presentation.

THE FACTS ABOUT GRANOLA

Granola has been touted as a very healthy food. The facts are that "regular" granola has a very high fat content. Unfortunately, commercial granola is not only full of fat, but the fat is usually hydrogenated, which is very unhealthy. Look for low-fat granola or shop for granola in health food stores, where most are made with unhydrogenated fats.

SMOKY HOME FRIES

INGREDIENTS

Serves 2

2 large Idaho potatoes

6 slices bacon, minced

1 medium white onion, peeled
and small diced

1 medium green bell pepper,
seeded and small diced

2 tablespoons butter

⅛ teaspoon salt

⅛ teaspoon freshly ground
black pepper

1. Simmer the potatoes, skin on, in salted water 10 minutes. Drain and let cool.
2. Peel the potatoes and cut into ¼"-thick pieces.
3. Place the bacon in a medium skillet and cook over medium heat until crispy, about 10–12 minutes. Remove the bacon and leave the fat in the pan.
4. Turn the heat to medium-high and add the potatoes. Do not stir the potatoes right away. Allow them to brown well on one side, about 8–10 minutes, before turning them.
5. Turn the potatoes over and add the onion, bell pepper, and butter. Cook about 10 minutes or until all the potatoes are browned and the onions and peppers are soft, stirring occasionally. Add the crispy bacon and toss to mix. Season with salt and pepper and serve.

BELL PEPPERS—SPICY OR NOT?

Green bell peppers are actually underripe red or yellow bell peppers. Many people think that red bell peppers are hot and spicy. But these peppers are actually sweeter than their green counterparts and make a great addition in many dishes for both color and flavor. Do not fear red peppers! If they are spicy, they will be advertised as such.

GREEN EGGS AND HAM

INGREDIENTS

Serves 2

---

2 tablespoons butter

4 ounces smoked ham, chopped

6 large eggs, beaten

3 tablespoons store-bought pesto

⅛ teaspoon salt

⅛ teaspoon freshly ground black pepper

1. In a medium nonstick skillet, heat the butter over medium heat until it stops bubbling. Add the ham and sauté 1 minute.
2. Add the eggs and pesto and cook as you would scrambled eggs. Season with salt and pepper. Serve hot alone or on toast if desired.

 EGG-CELLENT FACTS

Eggs are a great source of protein and healthy omega-3 fatty acids. The anatomy of an egg is quite interesting. The white is actually like amniotic fluid that protects the chick. The yolk is the food that the chick eats inside the shell before hatching. The little white squiggly thing on the yolk (called the chalaza) is actually what would be the chick if the egg were fertilized.

KIELBASA AND EGGS WITH ONIONS

INGREDIENTS

Serves 2

---

2 tablespoons butter

1 medium white onion, peeled and sliced thin

4 ounces kielbasa, small diced

5 large eggs, beaten

⅛ teaspoon salt

⅛ teaspoon freshly ground black pepper

1. In a medium skillet over medium heat, melt the butter. Add the onion and cook until well browned and soft, about 5–7 minutes. Add the kielbasa and sauté 2 minutes.
2. Add the eggs and cook as you would scrambled eggs. Season with salt and pepper and serve with rye toast if desired.

 SCRAMBLED EGG SECRETS

The secret to fluffy scrambled eggs that are moist and not watery is to cook them over medium to low heat and constantly stir the eggs. Never add milk to scrambled eggs; this only makes them watery.

HOT GRAPE-NUTS WITH HONEY

INGREDIENTS

Serves 2

3 cups Grape-Nuts Cereal

4 cups soy milk

3 tablespoons honey

Combine all the ingredients in a small pot and heat over low heat about 6 minutes. Serve in bowls like oatmeal.

 SUPER SOY

Soy protein is perhaps the healthiest protein on the planet, and soy milk is a great way to get some. Look for soy milks that are lower in sugar and unflavored. Japanese-style soy milks are usually much less sweet than the Chinese-style milks, which are loaded with sugar. There is no lactose in soy milk, and it is a great milk substitute for cooking and baking.

CHAPTER 3

Sandwiches

CHIPOTLE CHICKEN CLUB SANDWICH

INGREDIENTS

Serves 2

4 tablespoons mayonnaise

1 teaspoon store-bought chipotle pepper purée

6 slices whole-wheat bread, toasted

½ medium ripe avocado, mashed into a paste

½ pound cooked chicken breast, thinly sliced

8 slices bacon, cooked until crispy

1 large ripe tomato, thinly sliced

3 or 4 lettuce leaves

1. In a small bowl, mix together the mayonnaise and chipotle pepper purée. Spread the spicy mayonnaise on one side of 4 slices of the bread.
2. Spread the avocado on one side of the remaining 2 slices of bread.
3. Build the sandwiches: top 2 of the mayo-spread bread slices with the chicken. Place an avocado-spread bread slice avocado-side down on top of each. Divide the bacon, tomato, and lettuce on top of each sandwich. Finish by placing 1 of the remaining mayo-spread slices of bread on top of each sandwich.
4. Place 4 toothpicks in each sandwich and slice into quarters.

 JOIN THE CLUB

A club sandwich is a triple-decker sandwich with a BLT component. Basically you can make anything into a club sandwich by putting a BLT on top of it. The classics are turkey or roast beef, but do not be confined to these basics. Any grilled fish, cold cut, or even vegetable works great.

SMOKED TURKEY AND BRIE

INGREDIENTS

Serves 2

2 tablespoons prepared cranberry sauce

4 tablespoons Dijon mustard

4 slices multigrain bread, toasted

½ pound thinly sliced smoked deli turkey

6 ounces soft Brie cheese, thinly sliced

2 large lettuce leaves

1. In a small bowl, mix together the cranberry sauce and mustard. Spread on one side of each slice of bread.
2. Build the sandwiches by layering the turkey, cheese, and lettuce and enjoy.

 DIJON MUSTARD

Dijon mustard is from the town of Dijon in France. This region has been famous for its smooth and light mustards, which are sometimes made with the local white wine. There are countless varieties of mustards from all over the world, and you should try as many as possible.

ULTIMATE SOFT-SHELLED CRAB SANDWICH

INGREDIENTS

Serves 2

Vegetable oil, for deep-frying

1 cup flour

1 large cold egg

1 cup cold water

2 teaspoons Old Bay Seasoning

¼ teaspoon salt

¼ teaspoon freshly ground
   black pepper

2 large soft-shelled crabs

2 soft buns (such as hamburger
   buns or club rolls)

2 cups shredded iceberg lettuce

1 large ripe tomato, thinly sliced

2 lemon wedges

½ cup tartar sauce

1. Heat the oil in a large pot or deep-fryer to 375°F.
2. In a medium bowl, mix together the flour, egg, water, Old Bay, salt, and pepper. Do not overmix. Keep cold.
3. Dip the crabs in the batter and carefully place them in the oil. Fry about 5 minutes or until the oil stops bubbling and the crabs float, turning once. Transfer to paper towels to drain and blot dry.
4. Split the buns and lightly toast them. Place the lettuce and tomato on the buns and place the fried crabs on top. Squeeze the lemon over the crabs and top with tartar sauce.

 WORTH THE DEEP-FRY

The effort of deep-frying is well worth it with these crabs. It is such a treat to have a crab sandwich that many travel to Maryland just for the pleasure. These crabs are in season during spring and early summer, and they should be alive at the market.

SAUTÉED KIELBASA SANDWICHES

INGREDIENTS

Serves 2

¾ pound kielbasa, sliced into
   4"-long pieces about ¼" thick

4 slices rye bread with seeds

1 cup hot sauerkraut

3 tablespoons Polish-style
   mustard

1. In a small skillet over medium heat, sauté the kielbasa 1 minute per side.
2. Remove from pan and place the cooked kielbasa on 2 slices of the bread and top it with the sauerkraut, mustard, and remaining bread. Serve with plenty of cold beer and pickles.

 FLAVORS OF POLAND

The Poles are known for being expert sausage makers and meat smokers. Also popular in their cuisine are mustards, cabbages, caraway seeds, mushrooms, poppy seeds, and all manner of pork products. Try to seek out a Polish market and explore the rich and delicious foods of this nation.

CURRIED TUNA SALAD SANDWICH

INGREDIENTS

Serves 2

2 (6-ounce) cans tuna packed
   in water, drained

¼ cup chopped canned water
   chestnuts

2 scallions, finely minced

3 tablespoons mayonnaise

2 teaspoons sweet relish

1 tablespoon curry powder

⅛ teaspoon salt

⅛ teaspoon freshly ground
   black pepper

1 cup shredded lettuce

4 slices sourdough bread,
   toasted

1. Prepare the tuna salad in a medium bowl by mixing together the tuna, water chestnuts, scallions, mayonnaise, relish, curry powder, salt, and pepper.
2. Divide the shredded lettuce between 2 slices of the bread and pile the tuna salad on top. Top with the remaining bread and serve.

DECADENT PÂTÉ SANDWICH WITH SPICY ASIAN SLAW

INGREDIENTS

Serves 2

3 cups shredded napa cabbage

1 medium jalapeño pepper,
   seeded and minced

1 teaspoon minced fresh ginger

2 tablespoons granulated sugar

¼ cup rice vinegar

2 tablespoons chopped fresh
   cilantro

¼ teaspoon salt

2 soft hero rolls, split

8 ounces liver pâté or
   Braunschweiger liverwurst

1. In a large bowl, mix together the cabbage, jalapeño, ginger, sugar, vinegar, cilantro, and salt. Let stand 30 minutes, then drain.
2. Toast the insides of the rolls, spread with the pâté, and top with the slaw.

 CHOOSING PÂTÉ

Pâté is usually made from a combination of pork and duck livers. It is a very elegant item that exudes luxury. Look for pâtés that are smooth in texture, not the rough "country-style" pâtés, which are better eaten alone or on crackers. The silky texture of a fine pâté is what makes this sandwich so special.

TRUE CUBAN SANDWICH

INGREDIENTS

Serves 2

2 (8") soft hero rolls, split

¼ pound Swiss cheese, sliced

½ pound roast pork, thinly sliced

4 slices smoked ham

2 garlicky dill pickles, very thinly sliced

2 tablespoons melted butter

1 clove garlic, minced

1. Assemble the sandwiches by lining both sides of the rolls with the sliced cheese. Then pile on the pork, ham, and pickles. Close up the sandwiches.
2. In a small bowl, mix together the butter and garlic. Brush the garlic butter on all sides of the rolls.
3. Heat a large, heavy skillet over medium-low heat and place the sandwiches in the pan. Take another heavy pan and press it on top of the sandwiches to press them down while they grill. Turn them over when one side is well browned and the cheese begins to melt, about 3–4 minutes. Grill the other side and press again to really flatten out the sandwich. Serve hot.

 FINDING CUBANOS IN THE UNITED STATES

Anywhere that there is a Cuban neighborhood, you can find Cuban sandwiches, or Cubanos. The small local shops that cater to the working class are the best places to find these treats. Look for the telltale sandwich press, usually covered with aluminum foil, to tell you this treat is available. Order a Cubano with a café con leche and enjoy a truly Cuban delicacy.

GRILLED CHEESE WITH MAYONNAISE

INGREDIENTS

Serves 2

½ pound yellow American cheese, sliced

4 slices white bread

2 tablespoons mayonnaise

1. Assemble the cheese sandwiches by placing ¼ pound cheese on each of 2 slices of bread and topping with the remaining slices.
2. Spread the outsides of the bread with ½ tablespoon mayonnaise per slice and place in a medium nonstick pan over medium heat. Cook until both sides are crispy and brown, about 3–4 minutes per side. Serve immediately.

 UNCONVENTIONAL USES OF MAYONNAISE

Mayonnaise is made from oil and eggs, with oil being the dominant ingredient. Mayo can be used as a basting for a Thanksgiving turkey, or even as an oil substitute in a Caesar salad dressing. It's not just for sandwiches!

SMOKED SALMON AND CUCUMBER SANDWICH

INGREDIENTS

Serves 2

1 small cucumber, peeled and
  very thinly sliced

1 teaspoon salt

1 tablespoon white wine vinegar

1 teaspoon granulated sugar

¼ cup minced red onion

½ cup softened cream cheese

4 slices pumpernickel bread,
  toasted

1 large ripe tomato, thinly sliced

½ pound smoked salmon (lox)

1 teaspoon chopped fresh dill

1. Toss the sliced cucumber with salt and let purge 10 minutes. Squeeze the cucumbers dry, add to a small bowl, and toss with the vinegar and sugar.
2. In a separate small bowl, mix together the onion and cream cheese and spread on one side of all 4 slices of bread.
3. Top 2 slices of bread with 2 slices tomato, then the salmon and dill, then the cucumbers. Top off with the remaining bread and serve.

 COLD VERSUS HOT SMOKING

Smoked salmon (lox) is a cold-smoked product. This means that the temperature in the smoker does not reach a high enough temperature to cook the meat of the fish. Hot smoking is a process when the smoker is well over 140°F and the product gets fully cooked.

ROTISSERIE CHICKEN SALAD PANINI

INGREDIENTS

Serves 2

½ pound cooked rotisserie
  chicken, pulled apart roughly

2 tablespoons mayonnaise

1 teaspoon paprika

1 teaspoon garlic powder

1 teaspoon onion powder

¼ teaspoon salt

¼ teaspoon freshly ground
  black pepper

4 slices white or wheat bread

Cooking spray

1. In a medium bowl, mix together the chicken, mayonnaise, and all the spices. Pile onto the bread and make 2 sandwiches.
2. Spray the outside of the bread with cooking spray and toast in a medium skillet over medium heat 2 minutes per side.

 DRY SPICES VERSUS FRESH SPICES

In this recipe, onion and garlic powders are used instead of fresh onion and garlic. The reason this is sometimes done is that the flavor is desired but the texture of the ingredient is not. Do not substitute these items for fresh vegetables in soups or main dishes, but do experiment with them in spice blends and rubs.

MEXICAN-STYLE BEEF TORTA

INGREDIENTS

Serves 2

¾ pound trimmed skirt steak

2 tablespoons olive oil

1 teaspoon ground cumin

¼ teaspoon salt

¼ teaspoon freshly ground
   black pepper

2 large soft rolls, sliced

2 cups shredded iceberg lettuce

1 large ripe tomato, sliced

4–6 slices red onion

1 medium ripe Hass avocado,
   sliced

1 medium lime

Mexican hot sauce, to taste

1. Rub the steak with the oil, cumin, salt, and pepper. Place steak in a large skillet over medium-high heat and sear 3 minutes per side. Remove from pan and allow the meat to rest while you assemble the rest of the sandwich.

2. Pile one half of each roll with the lettuce, tomato, onion, and avocado. Squeeze the lime juice over the avocado.

3. Slice the meat across the grain into ¼" slices and pile on the rolls. Sprinkle with hot sauce, close up sandwiches, and enjoy.

 VIVA MEXICO!

Street food in Mexico is elevated to an art form. The streets are filled with all manner of carts and stalls offering everything from goat's head tacos to fresh fruit shakes. The most popular foods are the tacos and tortas. You will see many signs reading "Ricos Tacos" or "Ricos Tortas" all over Mexico. Here you can choose toppings and different meats to make your sandwich original.

GRILLED PEANUT BUTTER AND BANANA SANDWICH

INGREDIENTS

Serves 2

½ cup natural peanut butter

4 thick slices white bread

1 large banana, thinly sliced

3 tablespoons softened butter

1. Spread the peanut butter on one side of 2 slices of the bread, top each with the banana slices, and finish with the remaining slices of bread. Spread the outside of all the bread slices with the softened butter.

2. Place each sandwich in a medium nonstick pan over medium heat. Fry on both sides until well browned and the peanut butter is oozy and hot, about 3–4 minutes per side.

 GO USA!

Peanut butter was invented in the United States and was used as a high-protein/calorie food for our troops in their rations in both World Wars. It gained much popularity when the troops returned home and has been a favorite ever since. Try to seek out natural peanut butter.

SAUTÉED SALMON CLUB WITH SPICY MAYONNAISE

INGREDIENTS

Serves 2

---

2 (6-ounce) thin salmon fillets

1 tablespoon olive oil

¼ teaspoon salt

¼ teaspoon freshly ground black pepper

4 tablespoons mayonnaise

1 teaspoon Tabasco sauce

6 slices rye bread, toasted

6 slices bacon, cooked until crispy

4 romaine lettuce leaves

1 medium ripe tomato, thinly sliced

1. Rub the salmon with the oil and season with salt and pepper. Place salmon in a medium skillet over medium-high heat and sauté about 3 minutes per side or until the fish is just cooked. Set aside.

2. In a small bowl, mix together the mayonnaise and Tabasco; spread on one side of all the bread slices.

3. Top 2 of the slices of bread with the bacon, lettuce, and tomato. Top each with another slice of bread, then the salmon, and another slice of bread. Slice the triple-decker into quarters and serve.

 THE FUSS ABOUT SALMON

Salmon has gotten a lot of press recently, both negative and positive. The crux seems to be that salmon is rich in omega-3 fatty acids, which are a very healthy form of fat. However, the majority of salmon served in the United States is farm raised, and may contain higher than desirable levels of toxins because of conditions in the farms. Continue to enjoy salmon, but in moderation, perhaps two or three times a month.

PEANUT BUTTER AND BACON

INGREDIENTS

Serves 2

½ cup peanut butter (preferably natural)

4 slices white bread

8 slices bacon, cooked until crisp

Spread the peanut butter on one side of 2 slices of the bread and top with the cooked bacon. Close up the sandwiches and revel in the complex play of flavors and textures.

 WHY IT WORKS

Peanut and peanut-based sauces are common in many cultures and are often served in a savory and not sweet style. The famous satays of Asia, the African peanut soups, and the Chinese peanut-flavored dishes are just a few examples of the savory use of peanuts. Try it for yourself in this sandwich!

NEW YORK-STYLE ITALIAN COMBO SUBMARINE

INGREDIENTS

Serves 2

---

6 tablespoons extra-virgin olive oil

4 tablespoons red wine vinegar

2 teaspoons dried oregano

2 long submarine rolls, split almost all the way through

3 cups shredded iceberg lettuce

1 medium ripe tomato, thinly sliced

½ cup jarred roasted red peppers, drained and rinsed

4 ounces prosciutto, thinly sliced

4 ounces mortadella, thinly sliced

4 ounces capicola ham, thinly sliced

4 ounces provolone cheese, sliced

1. In a small bowl, mix together the oil, vinegar, and oregano; drizzle on the insides of the rolls. Pile the lettuce, tomato, and roasted peppers into each roll.
2. Add the meats and cheese equally to each of the sandwiches by folding each slice and nesting them inside of each other.

WHAT'S IN A NAME?

Different parts of the country have different names for the long sandwich on a roll referred to here as a submarine. In New England, the term is *grinder.* In many parts of the country the term is *hero,* and in Philly and New York, the term is *submarine.* Whichever name you use, the sandwiches are all delicious.

CHAPTER 4

Appetizers and Snacks

WATERMELON AND FETA CHEESE NUGGETS

INGREDIENTS

Serves 2

10 (2") cubes seedless
  watermelon

¼ cup finely minced red onion

5 Moroccan oil-cured olives,
  pitted and finely minced

1 tablespoon extra-virgin olive
  oil

½ cup crumbled feta cheese

10 small fresh mint leaves

1. Dig a small hole in each watermelon cube about ¾ of the way down into the flesh. A melon baller works great for this. (Basically you want to create a cavity to fill.)
2. In a small bowl, mix together the onions, olives, and oil. Place a small amount in each watermelon cube, filling each about halfway.
3. Fill the cavities the rest of the way with the crumbled feta and top each cube with a mint leaf. Serve as a finger food.

JAPANESE SPICY TUNA TARTAR

INGREDIENTS

Serves 2

1 cup vegetable oil

20 wonton skins

¾ pound sushi-grade tuna, cut
  into the smallest dice possible

2 scallions, sliced as thinly as
  possible

1 tablespoon soy sauce

Juice of ½ medium lime

1 teaspoon sriracha sauce (or
  hot sauce of your choice)

1 teaspoon sesame oil

1 teaspoon finely chopped
  pickled ginger

20 large shiso leaves or basil
  leaves

1. Heat the vegetable oil in a small skillet until barely smoking. Fry the wonton skins until they are golden brown and crispy, about 1 minute. Transfer to paper towels to drain.
2. Combine all the remaining ingredients except the shiso leaves (or basil) in a medium bowl and let marinate in the refrigerator 30 minutes or up to 1 hour.
3. When ready to serve, top each wonton skin with a shiso leaf and place a healthy-sized spoonful of the tuna tartar mixture on top of each. Place 10 on each plate and serve. (You eat these with your fingers, like you would a fancy canapé.)

 FINDING INGREDIENTS
You can find pickled ginger, wonton skins, and sriracha sauce in most ethnic sections of large supermarkets. Another place to look is in Asian-owned fish markets.

LIME AND CILANTRO-SCENTED CRAB SALAD

INGREDIENTS

Serves 2

2 tablespoons plus 2 teaspoons extra-virgin olive oil, divided

1 medium unripe Hass avocado, peeled and cut into chunks

2 tablespoons whole fresh cilantro leaves, divided

½ pound jumbo lump crabmeat, picked through for bits of shells, but pieces left as large as possible

Juice of 1 medium lime

½ teaspoon seeded and finely chopped jalapeño pepper

¼ teaspoon kosher salt

¼ teaspoon freshly ground black pepper

2 medium red radishes, sliced

3 grape or cherry tomatoes, sliced in half lengthwise

1. In a small skillet, heat 1 tablespoon of the olive oil until barely smoking. Add the avocado and sauté over high heat 1½ minutes, tossing gently. Transfer the avocado to paper towels and let cool to room temperature.

2. Roughly chop 1 tablespoon of the fresh cilantro leaves. In a medium bowl, gently toss the chopped cilantro with the crabmeat, 1 tablespoon olive oil, lime juice, jalapeño, salt, and pepper.

3. Firmly pack half of the crab salad into a ring mold placed in the center of a serving plate. (If you don't have a ring mold, you can use a tuna can with both the top and bottom removed.) Remove the mold and repeat with the remaining crab salad on another serving plate.

4. Arrange the radish slices on top of the crab salad. Place the tomatoes around the crab salad in a starburst fashion, cut-side down. Arrange the avocado chunks on the plates in a random fashion. Drizzle the plates with remaining 2 teaspoons olive oil and sprinkle with the whole cilantro leaves.

 BUYER BEWARE

Don't be afraid to ask to inspect the crab before buying it. Some unscrupulous packers fill the crabmeat tubs with shredded crab and place the nice big lumps on the top of the container to fool the consumer.

LUXURIOUS MANGO-LOBSTER SALAD

INGREDIENTS

Serves 2

1 medium ripe avocado, cut in
   half lengthwise and pitted
   (leave the skin on)

½ teaspoon salt, divided

½ teaspoon freshly ground
   black pepper, divided

½ medium lemon, zest grated

½ pound cooked lobster meat,
   diced

1 medium ripe mango,
   peeled and cut into thin,
   quarter-sized pieces

1 small shallot, peeled and
   finely minced

1 teaspoon chopped fresh
   tarragon

2 tablespoons extra-virgin
   olive oil

1. Season the avocado with ¼ teaspoon each salt and pepper, and rub the flesh with the lemon half to keep it from browning.

2. In a medium bowl, toss the lobster meat with the lemon zest, mango, shallot, tarragon, oil, and remaining salt and pepper.

3. Stuff the lobster mixture inside the cavity of the avocado, allowing it to spill over slightly for an abundant presentation. Serve immediately.

 THE PITS

To remove the pit from an avocado, simply cut the avocado in half lengthwise, twist the halves apart, and gently drive the blade of your knife into the pit. Twist the pit slightly, and knock the pit off of the knife into the garbage. Your fingers never even need to touch the pit.

GUACAMOLE

INGREDIENTS

Serves 2

1½ tablespoons lemon juice

¼ teaspoon sea salt

1 small ripe avocado

2 tablespoons finely chopped
   red onion

½ medium tomato, chopped

2 tablespoons sour cream

⅛ teaspoon freshly ground
   black pepper

1. In a medium bowl, combine lemon juice and salt and stir to dissolve salt. Cut avocado in half, remove pit, then peel and place in bowl with lemon-juice mixture; toss to coat. Mash avocado using a fork; make the mixture as smooth or chunky as you like.

2. Stir in onion, tomato, sour cream, and pepper and mix well. Serve immediately or cover by placing plastic wrap directly on the surface of the guacamole and refrigerate 20–25 minutes.

SCALLOP, CORN, AND OYSTER MUSHROOM SALAD

INGREDIENTS

Serves 2

Extra-virgin olive oil, as
  needed

½ pound scallops, patted dry

¼ teaspoon salt, divided

¼ teaspoon freshly ground
  black pepper, divided

½ pound oyster mushrooms,
  tough stems removed and
  caps torn into strips

3 ears corn, shucked and kernels cut off the cob

½ medium red onion, peeled
  and finely minced

2 small plum tomatoes, seeded
  and diced

¼ cup roughly chopped fresh
  flat-leaf parsley

1 tablespoon red wine vinegar,
  plus extra for dressing

2 cups endive lettuce or
  baby spinach

1. Add enough of the oil to a medium sauté pan to just coat the bottom. Heat over medium heat until barely smoking.

2. Add the scallops in a single layer, being sure not to crowd the pan. Season with half of the salt and pepper. Cook the scallops about 2 minutes, turning them only once when browned on the first side. Transfer to a plate immediately and place in the refrigerator to cool uncovered.

3. Wipe out the pan and add enough oil to just coat the bottom of the pan. Heat over medium heat until barely smoking, then add the oyster mushrooms. Cook the mushrooms about 4 minutes or until the water that is released from the mushrooms evaporates. Remove from heat and let cool.

4. In a medium bowl, toss together the cooled scallops along with any accumulated juices, the cooled mushrooms, the raw corn, onion, tomatoes, parsley, and vinegar.

5. Lightly dress the greens with a dash of oil and vinegar and sprinkle with remaining salt and pepper. Arrange the greens in the center of large serving plates. Equally divide the scallop salad over the greens and enjoy.

NO NEED TO COOK!

Raw corn is an amazing treat when the corn is in peak season. Do not hesitate to take a nibble at the market to assure that your corn is sweet, tender, and juicy. To remove the kernels from the cob, cut the ear in half, stand each half on your cutting board one at a time, and simply run your knife between the cob and the kernels. The kernels will fall right off.

DUCK BREAST "SUSHI" WITH PLUM SAUCE

INGREDIENTS

Serves 2

1 cup uncooked short-grain
 rice

2 cups cold water

2 tablespoons rice vinegar or
 apple cider vinegar

2 tablespoons granulated sugar

1 tablespoon minced pickled
 ginger

2 scallions, sliced as thinly as
 possible on a bias, divided

1 (6–8-ounce) duck breast

4 tablespoons prepared
 Chinese plum sauce or hoisin
 sauce

1. Place the rice and the water in the smallest pot available. Bring to a boil, then immediately turn down to a low simmer. Cover and cook 18 minutes. Once cooked, place in a large mixing bowl and break up with chopsticks or a fork.

2. Add the vinegar, sugar, and ginger to the rice and mix gently until the rice reaches room temperature, about 15 minutes. Stir in half the scallions and keep the rice at room temperature.

3. Score the skin of the duck breast in an X pattern. Place the duck breast skin-side down in a medium sauté pan with ¼" water. Bring to a gentle simmer and cook until the water boils off completely. Continue to cook the duck breast skin-side down over medium heat until the skin is golden brown and it begins to crisp.

4. When the skin is brown, flip the duck breast over and cook the flesh side approximately 2 minutes. Remove the duck from the pan and let cool in the refrigerator about 15 minutes.

5. Take small bunches of rice (about the size of a small egg) and gently form them into rectangles about 2" long, 1" wide, and 1" high (sushi shape). The rice should hold together but not be too firmly packed. Lay the rice bunches on a platter as you go, or divide between two serving plates.

6. Slice the duck breast straight across so the slices are about ⅛" thick and about the same size as the rice rectangles. Place a small dollop of plum sauce on the top of each rice rectangle, drape the duck meat over the top, and top with another dollop of plum sauce. Sprinkle the remaining scallions over the top.

CHICKEN AND LETTUCE WRAPS

INGREDIENTS

Serves 2

½ pound skinless, boneless
   chicken breast

1 tablespoon plus ⅛ teaspoon
   salt, divided

1 bay leaf

2 tablespoons mayonnaise

1 tablespoon roughly chopped
   toasted walnuts

2 teaspoons chopped fresh dill

⅛ teaspoon freshly ground
   black pepper

6 large leaves red leaf lettuce

¼ medium lemon

2 teaspoons extra-virgin
   olive oil

1. Fill a medium pot with 1 quart cold water. Add the chicken breast, 1 tablespoon salt, and bay leaf. Bring to a boil. As soon as the water boils, turn off the heat and allow the chicken to poach until a thermometer inserted in the thickest part of the chicken reads 165°F, about 6 minutes.

2. Remove the chicken from the pot and place on a plate in the refrigerator. Let cool at least 30 minutes. When the chicken is cool, dice into very small pieces, about the same size as the walnut pieces.

3. In a medium bowl, mix together the chicken, mayonnaise, walnuts, and dill. Season with remaining salt and pepper.

4. Divide the chicken mixture equally between the 6 lettuce leaves and roll the leaves into little spring rolls. Trim the lettuce leaves so there is no excess. Arrange 3 rolls on each plate, squeeze the lemon over them, and drizzle the oil over the top.

 PINK CHICKEN

Sometimes chicken appears pinkish even after it has been cooked to 165°F. This is due to the hemoglobin in the chicken, and sometimes has to do with the feed that the chickens are given. As long as an accurate thermometer reads 165°F, the chicken is safe to eat.

SHRIMP WITH ARUGULA PESTO

INGREDIENTS

Serves 2

———

1 cup roughly chopped arugula
   leaves (or spinach)

1 clove garlic, smashed

¼ cup toasted walnuts

2 tablespoons grated Parmesan
   cheese

¼ cup extra-virgin olive oil

¼ teaspoon salt, divided

¼ teaspoon freshly ground
   black pepper, divided

¾ pound (16–20) raw shrimp,
   heads and shells on

¼ cup dry white wine

1. To make the pesto, combine the arugula, garlic, walnuts, cheese, and oil in a blender or food processor. Blend until smooth, then season with half of the salt and pepper.

2. Heat a medium heavy skillet, preferably cast iron, over medium-high heat until a drop of water skates across the surface. Season the shrimp with the remaining salt and pepper and place in the pan in a single layer. Do not stir right away. Allow the shells to blister and burn a bit, about 1 minute. Toss the shrimp around in the pan or turn over onto the uncooked side and repeat the process until the shells are a bit charred and blistered and the shrimp are pink.

3. Add the white wine and toss with the shrimp. Cook until the wine has completely evaporated. (The entire cooking time should be around 3 minutes.)

4. To serve, toss the hot shrimp with the pesto and place in two bowls. To properly eat, twist the heads off the shrimp, then eat the entire shrimp, shell and all. (The shells impart a subtle smoky flavor.) You can also peel and eat if you prefer.

 SHELLS AND ALL
Cooking shrimp with their shells on has its benefits. First, the shell keeps valuable moisture inside the shrimp. Second, the shell itself provides a great deal of flavor on its own, especially if slightly burned or charred.

"FRICO" CHEESE CRISPS WITH ONIONS AND MUSHROOMS

INGREDIENTS

Serves 2

5 tablespoons extra-virgin olive oil, divided

1 (10-ounce) package white mushrooms, sliced

¼ teaspoon salt, divided

¼ teaspoon freshly ground black pepper, divided

1 tablespoon balsamic vinegar

2 tablespoons butter

1 large Spanish or white onion, peeled and thinly sliced

1 cup grated Montasio cheese

1 tablespoon chopped fresh parsley

1. Heat a 10"–12" sauté pan over medium-high heat, add 2 tablespoons oil, and heat until barely smoking.

2. Add the mushrooms and increase heat to high. Sauté the mushrooms until any water that releases from them has evaporated, about 4 minutes. Season with half of the salt and pepper, then add the balsamic vinegar. Cook about 30 seconds or until the mushrooms absorb the vinegar. Transfer the mushrooms to a bowl and keep warm.

3. Wipe out the same pan and reheat over medium-high. Add 2 tablespoons oil and all the butter. Heat until the butter stops bubbling, then add the onions. Season with remaining salt and pepper and cook, stirring occasionally, until the onions turn a deep brown color and start to look a bit "melted," about 10–15 minutes. When the onions are deeply caramelized, add them to the mushrooms. Keep warm.

4. Heat a small nonstick skillet (a 6" skillet is a good size) over medium heat. Brush the pan with ½ tablespoon oil. Sprinkle ½ cup cheese in the pan, covering the entire surface. The cheese will begin to melt, then bubble, and then come together as a mass. Check the underside to see when it starts to become golden. Just as the cheese begins to turn a golden color, spread half of the mushroom-onion mixture on top.

5. Cook 1–2 more minutes, then slide the frico onto a platter. Keep it warm. Repeat the process to make the second frico.

6. When ready to serve, use a spatula to carefully fold each frico in half onto a plate, much like an omelet. Sprinkle with the parsley and serve immediately.

 FRICO OUT!

If you are having difficulty finding the Montasio cheese called for in this recipe, you can substitute any semisoft cow's milk cheese, such as fontina. I recommend tracking down the Montasio, though—for the real deal.

MUDDA'S MINI MEATBALLS

INGREDIENTS

Serves 2

½ cup plain bread crumbs

¼ cup milk

¾ pound ground beef (or ¼ pound beef, ¼ pound veal, ¼ pound pork)

1 large egg, lightly beaten

½ cup grated pecorino Romano cheese

2 cloves garlic, smashed

3 tablespoons chopped fresh parsley

Pinch red pepper flakes

¼ teaspoon salt

¼ teaspoon freshly ground black pepper

¼ cup extra-virgin olive oil

1 (24-ounce) jar marinara sauce

1. In a small bowl, soak the bread crumbs in the milk 10 minutes.
2. Mix the bread crumbs with all the remaining ingredients except the olive oil and marinara. Roll the mixture into 1" balls and chill in the refrigerator 1 hour.
3. In a large skillet over medium heat, heat the olive oil until barely smoking and brown the meatballs well, about 2 minutes per side.
4. Transfer the meatballs to a medium saucepan along with the marinara sauce. Cook 30 minutes over medium heat. Enjoy on their own with toothpicks or with your favorite pasta as a meal.

MELON AND AVOCADO COCKTAIL

INGREDIENTS

Serves 2

1½ tablespoons extra-virgin olive oil

1 tablespoon raspberry vinegar, divided

1 teaspoon honey

⅛ teaspoon ground ginger

⅛ teaspoon sea salt

1 small ripe avocado, pitted and peeled

½ small cantaloupe, peeled and seeded

1. In a medium bowl, combine olive oil, ½ tablespoon vinegar, honey, ginger, and salt; mix well with wire whisk.
2. Cut avocado into chunks or make balls using a melon baller. Sprinkle remaining ½ tablespoon vinegar over prepared avocado.
3. Use a melon baller on cantaloupe to make small balls. Place cantaloupe and avocado in a serving bowl and drizzle raspberry vinegar dressing over all. Serve immediately.

HOW TO RIPEN AVOCADOS

The avocados you buy in the store are almost always rock hard, so purchase them a few days in advance. To ripen, store them together in a closed paper bag on the kitchen counter, checking every day to see if the flesh gives when gently pressed.

PROSCIUTTO AND AVOCADO WITH HAZELNUT VINAIGRETTE

INGREDIENTS

Serves 2

1 medium ripe Hass avocado

½ teaspoon freshly ground black pepper, divided

⅓ pound thinly sliced prosciutto

2 tablespoons toasted and crushed hazelnuts

1 tablespoon extra-virgin olive oil

1 tablespoon hazelnut or walnut oil

2 tablespoons red wine vinegar

2 tablespoons chopped fresh parsley

¼ teaspoon salt

1 cup loosely packed arugula leaves

1. Cut the avocado in half lengthwise and remove the pit with a knife. Peel the skin gently away and cut out any bruised portions. Cut the avocado lengthwise into ½" slices and season them with ¼ teaspoon pepper. Loosely wrap each avocado slice in a slice of prosciutto.
2. Make the dressing in a small bowl by mixing together the hazelnuts, oils, vinegar, parsley, and salt and remaining pepper.
3. Arrange the arugula leaves on two plates as a bed. Arrange the prosciutto-wrapped avocado across the plates and spoon the dressing over each piece of avocado.

 DIFFERENCES IN AVOCADOS

There are usually two kinds of avocados offered in the United States: bacon and Hass. The bacon avocados are much larger, are light green in color, and have a smooth skin. They also have less fat and more water. The Hass avocados are smaller and darker in color, have a pebbly skin sometimes with a purplish hue, and have a much richer, less watery flesh. They originated in California, first grown (and named) by Rudolph Hass.

SAUTÉED PARMESAN

INGREDIENTS

Serves 2

½ pound Parmigiano-Reggiano cheese

All-purpose flour, as needed

Extra-virgin olive oil, as needed

1 medium lemon

1 cup whole fresh basil leaves

1. Cut the cheese into chunks about ¼" thick, in the longest pieces possible. Dredge each piece of cheese in flour.
2. Heat about ½" olive oil in a small skillet over medium heat and sauté the cheese pieces about 30 seconds per side. They should be golden brown.
3. Squeeze the lemon over the cheese and use the basil leaves to pick up the morsels. Eat the leaf and the cheese together.

CHAPTER 5

Soups

MISO SOUP WITH SHRIMP

INGREDIENTS

Serves 2

4 cups water

3 tablespoons miso paste with dashi added

½ pound raw medium shrimp, shelled and deveined

1 (12-ounce) box silken tofu, cut into ½" cubes

4 scallions, thinly sliced

1. Bring the water to a boil in a medium stockpot; add the miso and whisk well.
2. Add the shrimp and simmer 3 minutes.
3. Divide the tofu and scallions between two bowls and pour the soup over them. Divide the shrimp equally between the bowls.

 MISO 101

Miso is a fermented paste made mostly from soybeans. It is a staple in Japanese cuisine. Dashi is a stock made from seaweed and bonito, which is a fish that is dried and often shaved into flakes. You can purchase miso with dashi added to simplify the soup. Otherwise, dashi powder can be purchased separately.

CANTONESE CRABMEAT AND EGG DROP SOUP

INGREDIENTS

Serves 2

4 cups chicken broth

1 (1") piece fresh gingerroot, peeled and smashed with the back of a knife

2 cloves garlic, thinly sliced

4 tablespoons soy sauce

½ pound fresh crabmeat, picked over for shells

2 cups baby spinach

3 tablespoons cornstarch dissolved in 3 tablespoons cold water

3 large egg whites, lightly beaten

2 scallions, thinly sliced

2 teaspoons sesame oil

1. In a medium saucepot, combine the broth, ginger, garlic, and soy sauce. Bring to a boil. Reduce to a gentle simmer and cook 10 minutes uncovered. Remove and discard the ginger.
2. Add the crabmeat and spinach and return to a boil. Very slowly drizzle in the cornstarch mixture while constantly stirring the soup. (It will slightly thicken the soup on contact.) Turn off the heat.
3. Stir the soup in one direction with a large spoon to make a whirlpool in the pot. While the hot soup is spinning, slowly drizzle in the egg whites; they will coagulate immediately. Let the soup stand 1 minute. Adjust seasoning with soy sauce if desired.
4. Divide into two warmed bowls and sprinkle with the scallions. Drizzle the sesame oil over the soup and serve.

BARBECUED BEEF AND BARLEY SOUP

INGREDIENTS

Serves 2

2 tablespoons vegetable oil

½ pound lean beef chuck, cut
  into ½" dice

1 small white onion, peeled
  and small diced

1 stalk celery, thinly sliced

1 small carrot, peeled and
  thinly sliced into rounds

6 white mushrooms, thinly
  sliced

2 teaspoons paprika

1 teaspoon garlic powder

1 teaspoon brown sugar

1 teaspoon dry mustard

⅓ cup dry pearl barley

½ cup canned diced tomatoes

1 (16-ounce) can beef
  consommé

3 cups chicken broth

1 tablespoon Worcestershire
  sauce

¼ teaspoon salt

¼ teaspoon freshly ground
  black pepper

1. Heat the oil in a medium saucepot over medium-high heat. Add the beef and brown well.
2. Add the onion, celery, carrot, mushrooms, paprika, garlic powder, sugar, and dry mustard. Sauté about 5 minutes or until the vegetables soften.
3. Add the barley, tomatoes, consommé, broth, and Worcestershire sauce. Bring to a boil, then reduce to a gentle simmer and cook 40 minutes uncovered.
4. Season with salt and pepper and serve in warmed bowls.

 CONSOMMÉ 101
A consommé is a stock that has been enriched with flavor and then clarified. A mixture of ground vegetables, meat, and egg whites—called a "raft"—is poached in the stock like a giant omelet, which flavors and clarifies the soup.

QUICK AND EASY MIDTOWN CLAM "CHOWDER"

INGREDIENTS

Serves 2

2 tablespoons vegetable oil

2 strips bacon, finely minced

1 small white onion, peeled and small diced

1 stalk celery, thinly sliced

1 small carrot, peeled and sliced into thin rounds

1 clove garlic, smashed

1 tablespoon fresh thyme

3 tablespoons all-purpose flour

1 (10-ounce) can baby clams, juice and clams separated

1 cup clam juice

3 cups chicken broth

1 tablespoon Worcestershire sauce

1 cup diced canned tomatoes

¾ cup peeled, small-diced Idaho potato

Dash Tabasco sauce

¼ teaspoon salt

¼ teaspoon freshly ground black pepper

1. In a medium saucepot, heat oil over medium-high heat and add the bacon, onion, celery, carrot, garlic, and thyme. Sauté until the vegetables soften, about 10 minutes.

2. Add the flour to the pot and stir well to avoid any lumps.

3. Add the juice from the canned clams plus the additional 1 cup clam juice, the broth, Worcestershire sauce, and tomatoes. Bring to a boil. Reduce heat to a gentle simmer and cook 20 minutes uncovered.

4. Add the potato and cook another 15 minutes uncovered or until the potato is tender.

5. Add the clams and a dash of Tabasco sauce. Heat the soup through, then season with salt and pepper. Serve in warmed bowls.

 WHAT MAKES A CHOWDER?

Classic chowder is not chowder unless it contains three essential ingredients: salt pork or bacon, potatoes, and milk or cream. This technically qualifies Manhattan clam chowder as a generic soup rather than a chowder. In Rhode Island they use both tomatoes and milk in the chowder to combine the best of both soups.

SMOKED TURKEY AND WILD RICE SOUP

INGREDIENTS

Serves 2

2 tablespoons butter (or
    extra-virgin olive oil)

1 small white onion, peeled
    and small diced

1 stalk celery, thinly sliced

1 small carrot, peeled and cut
    into rounds

2 cloves garlic, minced

1 bay leaf

1 teaspoon fresh thyme

¾ cup uncooked wild rice

½ pound smoked turkey meat,
    medium diced

5 cups chicken stock

¼ teaspoon salt

¼ teaspoon freshly ground
    black pepper

1. Heat the butter (or oil) in a medium pot over medium heat and add the onion, celery, carrot, garlic, bay leaf, and thyme. Sauté about 3 minutes until the vegetables begin to soften.
2. Add the rice and toss well with the vegetables to coat the grains with the fat.
3. Add the turkey meat and stock. Bring to a boil, then reduce to a gentle simmer. Cover and simmer 45 minutes or until the rice kernels start breaking open. Season with salt and pepper and remove the bay leaf. Serve in warmed bowls.

 TOASTING HERBS AND SPICES
When sturdy herbs and spices are tossed with hot fat in a pan, they release their essential oils and become even more fragrant and flavorful. This is a great way to maximize flavors.

BEEF AND TOMATO CHILI

INGREDIENTS

Serves 2

1 pound ground beef

½ cup chopped red onion

1 tablespoon all-purpose flour

2 tablespoons canned chopped
    jalapeños, undrained

1 (8-ounce) can tomato sauce
    with seasonings

1 cup canned diced tomatoes
    with garlic, undrained

½ cup water

1. In a large saucepan, cook ground beef and onion over medium heat, stirring frequently to break up meat, about 5 minutes. When beef is browned, drain off half of the liquid. Sprinkle flour over beef; cook and stir 2 minutes.
2. Add remaining ingredients, bring to a simmer, and simmer 10–15 minutes until flavors are blended and liquid is thickened. Serve immediately.

MEXICAN CHICKEN SOUP

INGREDIENTS

Serves 2

___

1 bunch fresh cilantro

2 skinless chicken thighs

5 cups chicken broth

1 small white onion, peeled
and medium diced

1 stalk celery, thinly sliced

1 small carrot, peeled and
sliced into thin rounds

½ cup corn kernels

3 cloves garlic, thinly sliced

2 teaspoons ground cumin

¼ teaspoon salt

¼ teaspoon freshly ground
black pepper

1 medium lime, cut in half

1. Separate the stems and leaves of the cilantro. Tie the stems in a bunch with twine and roughly chop the leaves. Set aside the leaves.
2. In a medium stockpot, combine the cilantro stems, chicken thighs, broth, onion, celery, carrot, corn, garlic, and cumin. Bring to a boil, cover, reduce heat to a gentle simmer, and cook 45 minutes.
3. Remove the cilantro stems and chicken. Discard the stems. Pull the chicken meat off the bones and cut into small pieces. Return the chicken to the pot.
4. Add salt, pepper, and cilantro leaves.
5. Serve in warmed bowls with a lime half beside each bowl. Squeeze the lime over the soup at the table.

QUICK CHINESE BROTH

INGREDIENTS

Serves 2

___

4 cups chicken stock

1 (3") piece fresh gingerroot,
peeled and smashed lightly

¼ cup soy sauce

1 teaspoon dashi powder (or
1 tablespoon dried bonito
flakes)

6 scallions

½ cup roughly chopped fresh
cilantro

Place all the ingredients except the cilantro in a medium stockpot and simmer gently over low heat 40 minutes uncovered. Strain the soup and add the cilantro. Drink hot.

 USING FISH FLAVORS IN UNUSUAL PLACES
The use of dried fish or dashi powder in this dish is a prime example of how fish and fish flavors are used in dishes that are not considered "fishy." Much like anchovy in a Caesar dressing, the dried fish adds a salty complexity without making the dish taste like fish. Most people who say they hate anchovy have never even tried one!

TUSCAN TOMATO AND BREAD SOUP

INGREDIENTS

Serves 2

½ cup extra-virgin olive oil, divided

1 small red onion, peeled and medium diced

1 stalk celery, thinly sliced

1 small carrot, peeled and cut into thin half-moons

3 cloves garlic, minced

2 cups canned diced tomatoes and their juice

3 cups chicken or vegetable broth

1½ cups cubed stale crusty bread

¼ teaspoon salt

¼ teaspoon freshly ground black pepper

½ cup grated Parmigiano-Reggiano cheese

8 basil leaves, torn into rough pieces

1. Heat half the oil in a medium pot over medium-high heat. Add the onion, celery, carrot, and garlic. Sauté 5 minutes until the vegetables are tender.
2. Add the tomatoes and broth and simmer 15 minutes.
3. Add the bread and simmer another 15 minutes.
4. Whisk the soup until the bread dissolves and the soup thickens; add the salt and pepper.
5. Pour into two warmed bowls and top each bowl with the cheese. Drizzle with the remaining olive oil and top with the basil leaves.

 OLIVE OIL AS A SEASONING

In Italy olive oil is as essential for seasoning as it is for cooking. Soups, grilled meats and fish, and all manner of vegetables are drizzled with extra-virgin olive oil as a final step to finish the dish with the great fragrance and silky texture that this liquid gold provides.

(ALMOST) MOM'S CHICKEN SOUP

INGREDIENTS

Serves 2

2 large skinless, boneless
chicken thighs

1 small white onion, peeled
and medium diced

1 stalk celery, thinly sliced

1 small carrot, peeled and cut
into thin rounds

1 cup shredded green cabbage

5 cups chicken broth

¼ teaspoon salt

¼ teaspoon freshly ground
black pepper

3 tablespoons chopped fresh
dill

1 cup small cooked pasta, such
as stars or pastina

1. In a medium pot, combine all the ingredients except the dill and pasta. Bring to a boil, then reduce to a gentle simmer. Simmer 1 hour covered.

2. Remove the chicken thighs and break into bite-sized pieces. Return the meat to the pot. Adjust seasoning with additional salt and pepper if desired.

3. Add the pasta and dill to the pot. Heat through and divide between two bowls to serve.

TORTELLINI EN BRODO

INGREDIENTS

Serves 2

5 cups rich chicken or beef
broth

3 cups cooked cheese tortellini

⅛ teaspoon salt

⅛ teaspoon freshly ground
black pepper

1 cup freshly grated Parmesan
cheese

¼ cup chopped fresh parsley

Heat the broth in a medium saucepot over medium heat. Add the tortellini and cook for just a minute or so until warmed through. Season with salt and pepper. Pour into bowls and garnish with the cheese and parsley.

 THE IMPORTANCE OF BROTH

Store-bought broth is pretty respectable these days, but nothing beats a real homemade broth. Use plenty of meat scraps and veggies and avoid boiling your broth too vigorously. (This will cause it to be cloudy and greasy.) Cook the broth for at least 3 hours and freeze in portions for later use.

HEARTY LENTIL AND SAUSAGE SOUP

INGREDIENTS

Serves 2

1 cup balsamic vinegar

6 ounces garlic sausage, small diced

2 tablespoons butter (or extra-virgin olive oil)

1 small white onion, peeled and small diced

1 stalk celery, small diced

1 small carrot, peeled and small diced

2 cloves garlic, minced

1 bay leaf

2 cups brown lentils

5 cups chicken broth

⅛ teaspoon salt

⅛ teaspoon freshly ground black pepper

2 tablespoons chopped fresh parsley

1. In a small saucepan, reduce the balsamic vinegar over medium heat until about 2 tablespoons remain and it is very thick. Remove from heat and set aside.
2. In a soup pot, cook the sausage over medium heat until well browned. Leave the fat in the pan.
3. Add the butter (or oil) and heat over medium-high heat. Add the onion, celery, carrot, garlic, and bay leaf. Sauté about 3 minutes until the vegetables begin to soften.
4. Add the lentils and stir well. Add the broth. Cover and simmer 25 minutes.
5. Season with salt and pepper and remove the bay leaf. Ladle into warmed bowls. Sprinkle with the parsley and drizzle with the balsamic syrup.

PRIZE-WINNING CHILI

INGREDIENTS

Serves 2

¼ cup vegetable oil (or bacon fat)

1 large white onion, peeled and medium diced

4 cloves garlic, minced

1 medium green bell pepper, seeded and medium diced

¼ cup all-purpose flour

1 heaping tablespoon ground cumin

1 heaping tablespoon ground coriander

1 heaping tablespoon chili powder

1 heaping tablespoon paprika

1½ pounds beef chuck, cut into ½" cubes

1 cup canned diced tomatoes

4 cups beef broth

¾ cup dark beer

2 tablespoons Worcestershire sauce

1 teaspoon brown sugar

¼ square unsweetened chocolate

1. Heat oil in a large heavy pot over medium-high heat. Add the onion, garlic, and bell pepper. Sauté about 5 minutes until well softened.
2. Add the flour and the dry spices and sauté another 2 minutes.
3. Add the meat, tomatoes, broth, beer, Worcestershire sauce, and sugar. Simmer gently 1½ hours or until the meat is fork-tender.
4. Turn off the heat and add the chocolate. Melt into the stew, stirring to mix. Serve with rice or cornbread.

CHOCOLATE AND CHILI

Both chocolate and chili peppers share the birthplace of Mexico, and the flavors mix well. The original chocolate drink of ancient Mexico was not sweet at all and contained chili peppers, almonds, and cinnamon. The small amount of unsweetened chocolate added to this chili adds a level of complexity that is sublime.

1700s LAYERED COD "CHOWDA"

INGREDIENTS
Serves 2

---

1 cup heavy cream

½ cup clam juice

1 teaspoon fresh thyme

2 medium Idaho potatoes, peeled and thinly sliced

4 strips bacon, finely chopped

1 (1-pound) chunk cod fillet, about 1½" thick, cut in half

¼ teaspoon salt

¼ teaspoon freshly ground black pepper

1 bay leaf

1. In a small bowl, mix together the cream, clam juice, and thyme and pour about ¼ cup of the mixture into a small pot.
2. Place a layer of the potatoes in the bottom of the pot and sprinkle some bacon over the top. Place 1 slice of the cod on top. Season each layer with some salt and pepper. Repeat this process until all the ingredients are used. Pour the remaining cream mixture into the pot and set over low heat.
3. Add the bay leaf, cover the pot, and gently simmer about 25 minutes or until the potatoes are cooked.
4. Divide into two bowls and serve with oyster crackers or toast if desired.

"SOUPER" FAST BLACK BEAN SOUP

INGREDIENTS
Serves 2

---

3 tablespoons olive oil

1 ounce chorizo

1 small white onion, peeled and small diced

1 clove garlic, minced

1 teaspoon dried oregano

½ cup corn kernels

1 (15.5-ounce) can black beans, drained and rinsed

4 cups low-sodium chicken broth

¼ teaspoon salt

¼ teaspoon freshly ground black pepper

2 tablespoons sour cream

1. Heat oil in a small saucepot over medium heat until barely smoking. Add the chorizo, onion, garlic, and oregano. Sauté until the onions have softened, about 3 minutes.
2. Add all the remaining ingredients except the sour cream and bring to a boil.
3. As soon as the soup boils, reduce to a low simmer and cook 15 minutes uncovered. Season with additional salt and pepper if desired.
4. Divide into two warmed bowls and top each with a dollop of the sour cream.

CHAPTER 6

Salads and Dressings

ENDIVE, WALNUT, AND BLUE CHEESE SALAD

INGREDIENTS
Serves 2

3 cups chiffonaded endive

2 tablespoons hazelnut oil

2 teaspoons apple cider vinegar

2 tablespoons finely minced fresh chives

⅛ teaspoon salt

⅛ teaspoon freshly ground black pepper

½ cup crumbled blue cheese

6 cherry or grape tomatoes, cut in half

½ cup toasted walnut halves

1. In a medium bowl, toss the endive with the hazelnut oil, vinegar, chives, salt, and pepper. Arrange in the center of a large salad plate.
2. Top with the blue cheese, tomatoes, and walnuts.

WHEAT BERRY SALAD

INGREDIENTS
Serves 2

1 cup wheat berries

½ cup minced scallions

¼ cup dried cranberries

¼ cup minced dried apricots

¼ cup toasted pistachios

2 tablespoons toasted pine nuts

¼ cup extra-virgin olive oil

3 tablespoons red wine vinegar

¼ teaspoon salt, plus more for water

¼ teaspoon freshly ground black pepper

1. In a small pot, boil the wheat berries in plenty of salted water 30 minutes. Drain and let cool.
2. Toss the wheat berries with the remaining ingredients in a medium bowl and let marinate in the refrigerator about 1 hour before serving.

 COMPLEX CARBS

Many people do not understand the difference between simple and complex carbohydrates. In a nutshell, simple carbs are usually refined and ground grains, like white flour, white rice, and pasta. These carbs burn quickly in the body and are not a very efficient fuel. Complex carbs, such as whole grains and brown rice, are much more efficient fuels for the body and are therefore much healthier.

SPICY CAESAR SALAD WITH CHIPOTLE DRESSING

INGREDIENTS

Serves 2

1 medium lime

¼ cup grated Parmesan cheese

2 anchovy fillets, rinsed and minced

2 cloves garlic, smashed

1 teaspoon Dijon mustard

2 tablespoons mayonnaise

1 teaspoon (or to taste) minced chipotle pepper in adobo sauce

¼ cup extra-virgin olive oil

⅛ teaspoon salt

⅛ teaspoon freshly ground black pepper

4 cups chopped romaine lettuce

½ cup chopped black olives

1 cup croutons

1. Juice the lime into a large mixing bowl. Add the Parmesan, anchovies, garlic, mustard, mayonnaise, and chipotle. Whisk together well. Slowly whisk in the olive oil in a slow stream. When incorporated, season with salt and pepper.

2. Add the lettuce and toss well. Place in the center of a large salad plate and toss the olives and croutons over the salad.

WHERE THERE'S SMOKE, THERE'S FIRE

Chipotle peppers are dried and smoked jalapeño peppers. They can be found in the Mexican section of the supermarket and are usually in small cans labeled "chipotle in adobo." Store the unused portion of the can in an airtight container in the fridge.

WARM SPINACH SALAD WITH DEVILED EGG CROUTONS

INGREDIENTS

Serves 2

3 large hard-boiled eggs, peeled and roughly chopped

1 tablespoon mayonnaise

1 teaspoon Dijon mustard

1 teaspoon paprika

¼ teaspoon salt

¼ teaspoon freshly ground black pepper

6 small slices (about 3" long and ½" thick, cut on the bias) baguette, toasted

8 strips bacon, cut widthwise into ¼" pieces

1 medium red onion, peeled and sliced into thin half-moons

1 cup sliced button mushrooms

6 cups baby spinach

1 cup diced ripe tomatoes

2 tablespoons red wine vinegar

1. In a medium bowl, mix together the eggs, mayonnaise, mustard, paprika, salt, and pepper. Crush with a fork until the egg pieces are no larger than peas. Divide the egg salad among the baguette croutons.

2. In a large sauté pan, cook the bacon over medium heat until very crispy. Be careful not to burn the fat. Transfer the bacon to paper towels to drain and leave the fat in the pan.

3. Add the onions and mushrooms to the bacon fat in the pan. Cook over medium-high heat until the moisture from the mushrooms has evaporated, about 4 minutes.

4. When the mushrooms are dry, add the spinach and tomatoes and remove the pan from the heat. Add the vinegar and toss very quickly to coat the greens with the dressing you have created in the pan.

5. Divide the salad between two plates. Crumble the bacon and sprinkle it over the salads. Place 3 croutons on each plate and serve immediately.

 TIME IS OF THE ESSENCE

The final steps of this salad demand speed. If the spinach remains in the pan too long, it will cook. The idea is to gently wilt the leaves in the warm dressing and slightly warm them. The time from the spinach hitting the pan to the plate should be about 45 seconds.

SAUTÉED MUSHROOM SALAD

INGREDIENTS
Serves 2

1 head butter lettuce (Boston
 lettuce), separated into
 leaves

½ pound mushrooms (such
 as porcini or chanterelles),
 cleaned and cut into ¼" slices

¼ cup plus 2 tablespoons
 extra-virgin olive oil, divided

¼ teaspoon salt

¼ teaspoon freshly ground
 black pepper

2 tablespoons balsamic vinegar

¼ pound thinly sliced prosciutto

¼ cup grated Parmigiano-
 Reggiano cheese

1. Arrange the tender inner leaves of the lettuce on two large salad plates, covering almost the entire surface.
2. In a medium skillet over medium-high heat, sauté the mushrooms in ¼ cup olive oil until the water they release has evaporated, about 4 minutes; season with salt and pepper. Keep warm.
3. Drizzle the lettuce leaves with 1 tablespoon balsamic vinegar and 1 tablespoon olive oil per plate.
4. Tear the prosciutto into bite-sized pieces and sprinkle it over the lettuce leaves. Top with the warm mushrooms and sprinkle with the cheese. Serve immediately.

WILD RICE SALAD

INGREDIENTS
Serves 2

½ cup wild rice

¼ cup extra-virgin olive oil

2 tablespoons apple cider vinegar

6 dried apricots, finely diced

¼ cup toasted pecans

1 cup baby spinach

3 scallions, finely sliced

2 teaspoons chopped fresh tarragon

¼ teaspoon salt

¼ teaspoon freshly ground black pepper

1. Cook the rice by boiling it in about 4 cups of salted water 45 minutes.
2. Drain the rice and while it is still hot mix in the oil and vinegar. Let cool in the refrigerator uncovered 1 hour.
3. Add the remaining ingredients and adjust seasoning with more salt and pepper if desired. Serve immediately.

 TARRAGON
Tarragon is not used very frequently in the United States. Its strong, licorice-like flavor is so assertive that some feel it has limited uses. It is nice in some chicken dishes and in some butter-based sauces. This salad benefits greatly from the small amount added.

WEDGE SALAD WITH CHUNKY RUSSIAN DRESSING

INGREDIENTS
Serves 2

½ large head iceberg lettuce

½ cup ketchup

½ cup mayonnaise

1 large hard-boiled egg, finely chopped

¼ cup finely minced red onion

¼ cup sweet relish

¼ cup capers, rinsed

1 tablespoon lemon juice

Dash Worcestershire sauce

Dash Tabasco sauce

1. Cut the iceberg into thick wedges and arrange on two plates.
2. Mix together all the remaining ingredients in a medium bowl.
3. Pour the dressing over the iceberg wedges and serve immediately.

 THE PERFECT BOILED EGG
Place large eggs in enough cold water to cover by 1" and bring to a boil. As soon as the water boils, turn off the heat. Let stand for 11 minutes. Drain, moving the eggs around a bit to crack the shells, then cool in ice water. Perfect every time. No green yolks or rubbery whites.

STALE BREAD PANZANELLA

INGREDIENTS

Serves 2

---

3 cups cubed sourdough bread
(about 2" cubes), left out
overnight

1 cup diced ripe tomatoes

1 small red onion, peeled and
finely minced

6 ounces fresh mozzarella
cheese, diced

½ cup extra-virgin olive oil

4 tablespoons red wine vinegar

½ cup shredded fresh basil

2 tablespoons capers, rinsed

¼ teaspoon salt

¼ teaspoon freshly ground
black pepper

Mix together all the ingredients in a large bowl and let stand at room
temperature 20 minutes. Adjust seasoning with salt and pepper
and serve.

 CHIFFONADE

To easily shred, or chiffonade, basil leaves, stack washed and
dried leaves on top of one another about six or seven at a
time and roll up lengthwise. Use a sharp knife to cut through
them all together. Make the slices as close to each other as
possible.

BABY POTATO AND STRING BEAN SALAD

INGREDIENTS

Serves 2

½ pound string beans, trimmed

½ pound new potatoes

1 tablespoon whole-grain
mustard

2 tablespoons apple cider vinegar

6 tablespoons vegetable oil

Pinch granulated sugar

6 slices bacon

2 tablespoons chopped fresh dill

¼ teaspoon salt

¼ teaspoon freshly ground
black pepper

1. Boil the green beans in plenty of salted water until crisp-tender,
   about 4 minutes. Cool in ice water and drain.
2. Boil the potatoes in salted water until tender, about 10 minutes.
   Drain and let cool. When the potatoes are cool enough to handle
   but still warm, peel off the skins and cut into slices about ¼" thick.
   Place the potato slices in a mixing bowl.
3. In a small bowl, mix together the mustard, vinegar, oil, and sugar.
   Pour over the warm potato slices and mix well. Spread out the
   potatoes on a plate and let cool in the refrigerator 30 minutes.
4. Slice the bacon into ¼" pieces and cook in a small pan over
   medium heat until crisp. Drain on paper towels.
5. When the potatoes are cool, add the green beans, bacon, and dill.
   Season with salt and pepper and serve.

TUNISIAN SALAD

INGREDIENTS

Serves 2

---

1 (15.5-ounce) can chickpeas, drained and rinsed

1 (6-ounce) can tuna packed in olive oil

2 anchovy fillets, minced

Juice of 1 medium lemon

4 scallions, thinly sliced

1 small cucumber, diced the same size as the chickpeas

8 cherry or grape tomatoes, quartered

¼ cup extra-virgin olive oil

1 teaspoon ground cumin

¼ teaspoon salt

¼ teaspoon freshly ground black pepper

Mix together all the ingredients in a large bowl and let marinate 1 hour in the refrigerator. Serve on chilled plates.

MOM'S CUCUMBER SALAD

INGREDIENTS

Serves 2

---

1 medium or 2 small cucumbers, sliced into thin rounds

¼ teaspoon salt

¼ teaspoon freshly ground black pepper

½ cup sour cream

2 tablespoons chopped fresh dill

1 clove garlic, smashed

1. Place the cucumbers in a colander and season with salt and pepper. Let drain 20 minutes.

2. Squeeze the cucumbers gently to get a bit more water out of them.

3. In a medium bowl, toss the cucumbers with the sour cream, dill, and garlic. Adjust seasoning if necessary with additional salt and pepper. Serve cold.

 MUTANT CUKES

Gardeners are always giving gifts of giant cucumbers in the summer. These veggies grow very large quickly. Unfortunately, the bigger the cuke, the less flavor it packs. Choose medium or small cukes for better flavor and texture.

CITRUS AND SESAME SOYBEAN SALAD

INGREDIENTS

Serves 2

8 ounces fresh shelled
    soybeans

1 sheet nori seaweed

1 medium orange, peeled and
    separated into sections

2 tablespoons soy sauce

1 tablespoon sesame oil

1 tablespoon toasted sesame
    seeds

¼ teaspoon salt

1. Boil the beans in salted water in a medium pot 5 minutes. Cool in ice water and drain.

2. Heat one of your burners to medium if it is electric, or light and set a medium flame if you have a gas. Toast the seaweed by passing it over the burner of your stove quickly on each side. The sheet will smell toasty and shrink slightly. Crumble the sheet into small pieces.

3. Mix together all the ingredients in a large bowl and let marinate in the refrigerator 1 hour. Add additional salt if necessary.

NECTARINE AND CUCUMBER SUMMER SALAD

INGREDIENTS

Serves 2

2 medium nectarines, cut into
    thin slices

1 small cucumber, small diced

½ small red onion, peeled and
    finely minced

2 tablespoons finely chopped
    fresh chives

3 tablespoons extra-virgin
    olive oil

1 tablespoon white wine vinegar

¼ teaspoon salt

¼ teaspoon freshly ground
    black pepper

Mix together all the ingredients in a large bowl and serve immediately.

DOMINICAN AVOCADO SALAD

INGREDIENTS

Serves 2

¼ cup extra-virgin olive oil

Juice of 1 medium lime

1 clove garlic, smashed

2 tablespoons finely chopped
fresh cilantro

1 teaspoon dried oregano

¼ teaspoon salt

¼ teaspoon freshly ground
black pepper

2 bunches watercress, large
stems removed

1 small ripe tomato, thinly
sliced

1 small red onion, peeled and
thinly sliced

1 small ripe Hass avocado

1. Make the dressing by whisking together the oil, lime juice, garlic, cilantro, oregano, salt, and pepper in a large bowl.
2. Add the watercress to the bowl, toss it with the dressing, then arrange in the center of two plates. Arrange the tomato and onion slices on top of the greens.
3. Cut the avocado in half and remove the pit. Scoop out the flesh and cut into ¼" slices. Place on top of the salad and season the avocado with additional salt and pepper if desired. Serve immediately.

TAKING THE BITE OUT OF ONIONS

When onions are too strong, slice them thinly and soak them in ice water for 10 minutes. This removes the bite and crisps up the onions nicely. Another option is to marinate the onions in a mixture of equal amounts of red vinegar and granulated sugar. Completely cover the onions in this mixture like pickles in brine. They will last for 2 weeks in the refrigerator.

CALAMARI AND RICE SALAD

INGREDIENTS

Serves 2

½ pound cleaned calamari rings

1 cup cooked and cooled white rice

1 stalk celery, thinly sliced

12 pimiento-stuffed olives, cut in half

½ cup loosely packed flat-leaf parsley leaves

⅓ cup extra-virgin olive oil

3 tablespoons white wine vinegar

¼ teaspoon salt, plus more for water

¼ teaspoon freshly ground black pepper

1. Bring a small pot of salted water to a boil, add the calamari rings, and boil exactly 2 minutes. Drain and chill the calamari in ice water. Drain and dry on paper towels.

2. In a medium bowl, mix together all the remaining ingredients and let marinate in the refrigerator 20 minutes before serving. (Leave the parsley leaves whole in this recipe—they act as a sort of green for the salad.)

 PARSLEY 101

For years every plate on earth it seemed was adorned with a sprig of curly parsley. This turned parsley into a garnish rather than the true ingredient it is. Use the flat-leaf parsley (also called Italian parsley) for its superior flavor and texture.

CHAPTER 7

Side Dishes

POTATO CROQUETTES WITH SMOKED GOUDA

INGREDIENTS

Serves 2

2 cups leftover mashed
   potatoes

1 large egg, lightly beaten

2 tablespoons all-purpose flour

¼ teaspoon salt

¼ teaspoon freshly ground
   black pepper

4 cubes smoked Gouda, about
   1" each

Olive oil, for frying

1. In a medium bowl, mix together the potatoes, egg, flour, salt, and pepper. Divide into 4 piles and form into loose balls.
2. Press a cube of cheese into the center of each ball and form into patties.
3. Heat about 1" olive oil in a large heavy pan over medium-high heat until almost smoking. Fry the patties about 2 minutes per side. Serve hot.

STRING BEANS WITH TOASTED BREAD CRUMBS

INGREDIENTS

Serves 2

2 tablespoons butter

1 clove garlic, minced

½ cup plain bread crumbs

4 cups snipped green beans

¼ teaspoon salt, plus more for
   water

¼ teaspoon freshly ground
   black pepper

1. Melt the butter in a small pan over low heat and add the garlic and bread crumbs. Cook, stirring occasionally, until the bread crumbs are well toasted and the butter releases a nutty aroma, about 3–4 minutes. Keep warm.
2. Boil the green beans in a large pot in plenty of salted water until tender, about 3–4 minutes. Drain and toss with the buttered bread crumbs. Season with salt and pepper and serve.

WILD MUSHROOM MASHED POTATOES

INGREDIENTS

Serves 2

---

2 large Idaho potatoes, peeled and cut into 2" cubes

1 tablespoon kosher salt

3 tablespoons butter, divided

½ pound mixed wild mushrooms, trimmed and sliced

1 clove garlic, minced

¼ teaspoon salt, divided

¼ teaspoon freshly ground black pepper, divided

½ cup half-and-half

1 tablespoon chopped fresh parsley

1. Place the potatoes in a medium pot and cover with cold water by 1". Add the kosher salt and bring to a very gentle simmer. Cook about 20 minutes or until the potatoes are fork-tender.
2. Meanwhile, heat 1 tablespoon butter in a medium pan over medium-high heat until it stops bubbling. Add the mushrooms, garlic, and half of the salt and pepper and sauté until the water that releases from the mushrooms evaporates, about 4 minutes. Remove from heat.
3. Drain the potatoes very well. Mash the potatoes with the remaining butter and the half-and-half. Season with remaining salt and pepper and fold in the mushrooms and parsley. Keep hot and serve.

 KEEPING MASHED POTATOES HOT

Here is a tip for keeping mashed potatoes hot for long periods of time. After the potatoes are finished, transfer them to a heatproof container and cover. Place the container in a pot filled with a few inches of water. Place the pot over a burner and heat the water until very hot, but don't let it boil.

BROCCOLI DI RAPE

INGREDIENTS

Serves 2

---

1 bunch broccoli raab

2 tablespoons extra-virgin olive oil

1 clove garlic, minced

Pinch red pepper flakes

2 tablespoons toasted pine nuts

2 tablespoons golden raisins

¼ teaspoon salt, plus more for water

¼ teaspoon freshly ground black pepper

1. Boil the broccoli raab in plenty of salted water 3 minutes. Cool in ice water and drain.
2. Heat the olive oil in a medium sauté pan over medium heat and add the garlic and red pepper flakes. Sauté until the garlic is golden, about 2–3 minutes. Add the pine nuts, raisins, and broccoli raab. Sauté until the broccoli is hot. Season with salt and pepper and serve.

 CULINARY HISTORY

The combination of raisins and nuts was brought to southern Italy by Arabs during the spice trade. This combination of sweet and savory is very popular in North Africa and most Arab countries. This same influence brought the widespread use of nutmeg to many Italian dishes.

CUMIN AND SWEET PEA BASMATI RICE

INGREDIENTS

Serves 2

---

1 cup basmati rice

2 tablespoons butter, divided

1 small white onion, peeled
   and finely diced

1 clove garlic, minced

1 teaspoon cumin seeds

½ cup baby peas

1½ cups chicken stock

¼ teaspoon salt

¼ teaspoon freshly ground
   black pepper

1. Wash the rice under cold running water until the water runs clear. Soak the rice in cold water 30 minutes.
2. In a medium saucepot, heat 1 tablespoon butter over medium heat and sauté the onion, garlic, and cumin seeds 3 minutes or until the onions are lightly golden.
3. Drain the rice, add it to the pot, and stir well. Add the peas and stock and bring to a simmer. Immediately reduce the heat to the lowest setting and cover the pot.
4. Cook exactly 15 minutes. Remove from heat and add the remaining butter and salt and pepper. Stir gently to avoid breaking the grains of rice. Serve immediately.

 CUMIN

A very characteristic seasoning popular in Indian, Arab, and Mexican cuisines, cumin is usually used ground. Here the whole seeds add a gentler perfume than if the ground seeds were used. You can also buy the seeds, toast them in a dry pan, and then grind them in a spice mill.

SAVORY MARINATED MUSHROOMS

INGREDIENTS

Serves 2

---

1 pound assorted mushrooms

1 cup sherry vinegar

½ cup granulated sugar

¼ cup extra-virgin olive oil

¼ teaspoon salt

¼ teaspoon freshly ground
   black pepper

1 tablespoon chopped fresh
   savory

Place everything except the savory in a small pan. Bring to a boil, then turn off heat and let cool to room temperature. Drain and toss with the savory.

 PICKLE IT

This technique of boiling a vegetable in vinegar and sugar is a very simple pickling process. You can try this with almost any vegetables and add any seasonings you wish. This is a great way to preserve vegetables that are overabundant in the garden. Pick up a book on preserving and pickling and have a ball!

PESTO RICE

INGREDIENTS

Serves 2

1 cup long-grain white rice

2 cups cold water

½ cup store-bought pesto

¼ teaspoon salt

¼ teaspoon freshly ground
 black pepper

½ cup halved cherry tomatoes

1. Place the rice and water in a small pot. Bring to a simmer over medium heat, then reduce heat to the lowest setting. Cover and cook exactly 18 minutes. Remove from heat and let sit 5 minutes covered.

2. Add the pesto to the rice and season with salt and pepper. Toss in the cherry tomatoes and serve.

MINTED SWEET PEAS

INGREDIENTS

Serves 2

1 cup shelled fresh peas (about
 1 pound unshelled)

¼ teaspoon granulated sugar

1 tablespoon butter

¼ teaspoon sea salt

⅛ teaspoon freshly ground
 black pepper

1½ tablespoons chopped fresh
 mint

In a medium skillet, simmer the peas and sugar over medium-high heat until bright green and tender, about 5 minutes; drain. Toss peas with butter, salt, pepper, and mint.

OLD-FASHIONED GLAZED CARROTS

INGREDIENTS

Serves 2

2 large carrots, peeled and cut
 into ¼" slices

2 teaspoons butter

2 tablespoons water

½ teaspoon granulated sugar

⅛ teaspoon sea salt

Combine all ingredients in a medium heavy-bottomed skillet. Set over medium-high heat and simmer about 5 minutes, then toss or flip the carrots. Continue cooking until the liquid is mostly evaporated and what remains is a glaze adhering to the carrots. Be careful not to go too far, or the glaze will break down and become oily.

BRAISED RED CABBAGE

INGREDIENTS
Serves 2

4 tablespoons butter, divided

1 large white onion, peeled and
thinly sliced

6 cups shredded red cabbage

1 medium Granny Smith apple,
peeled, cored, and roughly
chopped

2 tablespoons red wine vinegar

¼ cup granulated sugar

1 cup dry red wine

½ cup water

1 whole clove garlic, peeled

1 small cinnamon stick

¼ teaspoon salt

¼ teaspoon freshly ground
black pepper

1. Melt 2 tablespoons butter in a medium pot over medium heat
   and add the onion. Sauté the onion until it begins to soften,
   about 5–7 minutes. Add the remaining ingredients except the
   remaining butter.

2. Bring to a boil, then reduce heat to low and cover. Cook 1 hour
   and 15 minutes. Turn off heat and add the remaining butter.
   Remove garlic clove and cinnamon stick. Adjust seasoning with
   additional salt and pepper if necessary and serve.

 KEEP IT RED

Foods with red pigments, such as red cabbage and beets, will
keep their brilliant red color during cooking if a small amount
of acid is present. Add a bit of vinegar, wine, or lemon juice to
these vegetables and their color will fix. This is important for
presentation purposes.

RISI BISI

INGREDIENTS
Serves 2

1 tablespoon extra-virgin olive
oil

¼ cup finely chopped white
onion

½ cup long-grain white rice

1 cup chicken broth

¼ cup green peas

2 tablespoons grated Parmesan
cheese

1. In a medium heavy saucepan, heat olive oil over medium heat.
   Add onion; cook and stir until onion is translucent, about
   5 minutes.

2. Add rice; cook and stir 2 minutes. Add chicken broth and bring to
   a boil. Cover pan, reduce heat, and simmer mixture 15–20 minutes until rice is almost tender and liquid has evaporated.

3. Add peas, cover, reduce heat to medium-low, and cook until peas
   are hot and rice is tender, 3–5 minutes. Stir in cheese and serve.

HONEY-ORANGE CARROTS

INGREDIENTS

Serves 2

1½ cups baby carrots

1 cup water

1 tablespoon orange juice
  concentrate

1 tablespoon honey

1 tablespoon butter

⅛ teaspoon dried thyme

1. Rinse carrots and place in a medium saucepan with water. Bring to a boil over high heat, then lower heat to medium and simmer 5 minutes or until just tender. Drain carrots and return to pan.
2. Stir in orange juice concentrate, honey, and butter; cook and stir over medium heat until sauce thickens and coats carrots, about 2 minutes. Add thyme and simmer 1 minute, then serve.

BABY CARROTS

Baby carrots are actually large carrots that have been carefully trimmed and shaped. They are sweeter than the carrots you remember from your childhood because they are a different variety that is bred to grow faster, longer, and with a higher sugar content.

BARLEY RISOTTO WITH CARAMELIZED ONIONS

INGREDIENTS

Serves 2

2 tablespoons butter

1 large white onion, peeled and
  finely diced

½ cup pearl barley

½ cup dry white wine

4 cups chicken broth

½ cup grated Parmesan cheese

3 tablespoons chopped fresh
  parsley

¼ teaspoon salt

¼ teaspoon freshly ground
  black pepper

1. Heat the butter in a medium pot over medium heat and add the onion. Cook the onion until well browned, about 8–10 minutes. Add the barley and wine and cook until the wine evaporates.
2. Add the broth and simmer very gently until the barley is done, about 35 minutes.
3. Turn off the heat and stir in the cheese and the parsley. Season with salt and pepper and serve.

HERBED COUSCOUS

INGREDIENTS

Serves 2

1 tablespoon extra-virgin olive oil

¼ cup finely chopped white onion

½ cup chicken or vegetable broth

⅛ teaspoon dried oregano

⅛ teaspoon dried marjoram

⅛ teaspoon sea salt

¼ cup couscous

1. In a medium saucepan, heat olive oil over medium heat. Add onion; cook and stir until tender, about 4 minutes.
2. Add broth, herbs, and salt and bring to a rolling boil. Stir in couscous, then cover pan and remove from heat. Let stand 5 minutes or according to package directions until liquid is absorbed. Fluff couscous mixture with a fork and serve.

BROCCOLI TOSS

INGREDIENTS

Serves 2

2 cups broccoli florets

2 cups water

1 tablespoon extra-virgin olive oil

½ tablespoon butter

½ cup chopped white onion

2 cloves garlic, minced

1 tablespoon toasted sesame seeds

1. Place broccoli florets in a large saucepan and cover with water. Bring to a boil, then reduce heat and simmer uncovered 5 minutes until crisp-tender.
2. Meanwhile, place olive oil and butter in a medium skillet over medium heat. Add onion and garlic; cook and stir 4–6 minutes.
3. Drain broccoli thoroughly and add to skillet with onion and garlic. Toss broccoli with onion mixture. Sprinkle with sesame seeds, toss gently, and serve.

 ABOUT BROCCOLI

The trick to cooking broccoli is to use a large amount of water and cook it uncovered very quickly. Use at least 4 cups of water for each head of broccoli. Follow these steps and your broccoli will be crisp-tender and mildly flavored.

CHAPTER 8

Chicken Main Dishes

QUICK CHICKEN CACCIATORE WITH MUSHROOMS

INGREDIENTS

Serves 2

2 whole chicken legs, thighs attached

¼ teaspoon salt, divided

¼ teaspoon freshly ground black pepper, divided

All-purpose flour, as needed

8 tablespoons extra-virgin olive oil, divided

3 cloves garlic, sliced

1 small white onion, peeled and sliced

1 medium carrot, peeled and cut into thin half-moons

1 (10-ounce) package white mushrooms, sliced

1 cup dry red wine

1 cup chicken broth

1 (16-ounce) can crushed tomatoes

1 bay leaf

1 sprig fresh oregano (or rosemary)

1. Separate the chicken legs and thighs and season well with half the salt and pepper. Dust with flour and shake off the excess.

2. Heat 4 tablespoons oil in a large skillet over medium-high heat. Brown the chicken well on all sides, about 4 minutes per side. Remove the chicken from the pan and set aside.

3. Add the remaining oil to the same pan and add the garlic, onion, carrot, and mushrooms. Sauté 5 minutes or until the vegetables begin to soften.

4. Add the wine, broth, tomatoes, bay leaf, and oregano. Season with remaining salt and pepper. Return the chicken to the pan and bring to a gentle simmer. Cook partially covered 45 minutes or until the chicken is very tender and the broth has slightly thickened. Serve hot alone or over pasta or polenta if desired.

 HUNTERS' STEW

Cacciatore means "hunter" in Italian. Since hunters prowl the forest for their prey, and mushrooms inhabit these same woods, the term *cacciatore* will almost always signify the addition of mushrooms in a dish.

CHICKEN MEDALLIONS WITH SWEET SHERRY AND MUSHROOM SAUCE

INGREDIENTS

Serves 2

¾ pound skinless, boneless chicken breast, cut into thin 3" medallions

⅛ teaspoon salt

⅛ teaspoon freshly ground black pepper

All-purpose flour, as needed

3 tablespoons butter, divided

1 (10-ounce) package white mushrooms, sliced

¾ cup finely minced red onion

1 clove garlic, minced

½ cup sweet sherry, divided

1 cup jarred brown gravy

2 tablespoons minced fresh chives

1. Season the chicken with salt and pepper and dust with flour. Shake off any excess.

2. Heat 1½ tablespoons butter in a medium skillet over medium-high heat until it stops bubbling. Add the chicken and cook about 1 minute on each side until light golden. Transfer the chicken to a plate and keep warm.

3. Wipe out the pan, add the remaining butter, and cook over medium-high heat until it stops bubbling. Add the mushrooms, onion, and garlic. Sauté until the water released from the mushrooms evaporates, about 4 minutes.

4. Add half of the sherry and boil 1 minute. Add the gravy and bring to a simmer.

5. Return the chicken to the pan along with the remaining sherry and the chives. Cook about 3 minutes to heat through and serve.

 FORTIFIED WINE
Sherry is a fortified wine, which is wine that has had brandy added to it and is then aged to achieve a complex flavor. Other examples of fortified wines are port, Madeira, and marsala. All can be used interchangeably.

STIR-FRIED CHICKEN

INGREDIENTS

Serves 2

1 ounce dry sherry

5 tablespoons soy sauce, divided

4 teaspoons sesame oil, divided

½ pound skinless, boneless chicken thighs, cut into thin strips

6 tablespoons peanut oil, divided

1 small white onion, peeled and thinly sliced

3 scallions, thinly sliced

3 cloves garlic, minced

1 tablespoon grated fresh ginger

2 cups snow peas, julienned

½ cup chicken stock

2 tablespoons cornstarch dissolved in 2 tablespoons water

1. In a medium bowl, mix together the sherry, 3 tablespoons soy sauce, and 2 teaspoons sesame oil. Add the chicken and coat thoroughly in this mixture. Let marinate in the refrigerator at least 1 hour or up to overnight.

2. When ready, place 3 tablespoons peanut oil in a wok or cast-iron pan and heat over high heat until very hot. Add the chicken and stir-fry over high heat about 2 minutes. Transfer the chicken to a plate and set aside.

3. Wipe out the pan and add remaining 3 tablespoons peanut oil. Add the onion, scallions, garlic, ginger, and snow peas. Stir-fry about 1 minute.

4. Return the chicken to the pan. Add the remaining soy sauce and the chicken stock and bring to a boil. Let boil about 1 minute, then slowly stir in the cornstarch slurry until the sauce thickens. Turn off the heat, add the remaining sesame oil, and serve immediately.

 MAKE IT SNAPPY

There are three keys to a successful stir-fry. First, you must have a very hot pan or wok. Second, you must have all the ingredients ready to go and organized. Third, you must be able to move quickly, because once it starts, it is a very quick process.

CURRIED CHICKEN HOT POT

INGREDIENTS
Serves 2

1 tablespoon red curry paste

2 cups chicken broth

¾ pound skinless, boneless
chicken thighs, cut into 1"
chunks

1 cup coconut milk

1 tablespoon grated fresh ginger

10 scallions, white part only,
trimmed but left whole

6 ounces fresh lotus root, cut
into ½" slices

⅛ teaspoon salt

1 large ripe tomato, cut into
1" chunks

2 tablespoons chopped fresh
cilantro

1. In a small bowl, whisk together the red curry paste and the chicken broth to dissolve the paste.
2. In a medium pot, combine all the ingredients except the salt, tomato, and cilantro. Bring to a simmer over medium heat. Cover and simmer gently 25 minutes.
3. Season with salt, then add the tomato and cilantro. Serve in bowls.

CHICKEN VERONIQUE

INGREDIENTS
Serves 2

2 tablespoons all-purpose flour

¼ teaspoon sea salt

⅛ teaspoon freshly ground
black pepper

¼ teaspoon dried marjoram

2 (4-ounce) skinless, boneless
chicken breasts

2 tablespoons butter

½ cup chicken stock

¼ cup white grape juice

¾ cup red grapes, cut in half

1. On a shallow plate, combine flour, salt, pepper, and marjoram. Coat chicken breasts in this mixture. In a heavy skillet over medium heat, melt butter. Add chicken breasts and cook 4 minutes. Turn chicken over and cook 4–6 minutes longer until chicken is just done. Remove chicken from pan and cover with foil to keep warm.
2. Add stock and grape juice to pan and bring to a boil, scraping up pan drippings. Boil over high heat 6 minutes until sauce is reduced and thickened. Return chicken to pan along with red grapes and cook over low heat 2–3 minutes until grapes are hot and chicken is tender.

CHICKEN BREASTS IN LEMON SAUCE WITH DILL

INGREDIENTS

Serves 2

2 (6-ounce) skinless, boneless chicken breasts, slightly pounded

⅛ teaspoon salt

⅛ teaspoon freshly ground black pepper

¼ cup all-purpose flour, plus extra for dusting

4 tablespoons extra-virgin olive oil

2 tablespoons butter

2 cups chicken stock

¼ cup fresh-squeezed lemon juice

2 tablespoons chopped fresh dill

1. Season the chicken with salt and pepper and dust with flour. Heat the olive oil in a medium skillet over medium-high heat. Add the chicken and brown on both sides. Remove from pan and set aside.

2. In the same pan, melt the butter and stir in ¼ cup flour. When smooth, slowly add the stock, whisking well. Bring to a gentle simmer and cook 20 minutes uncovered.

3. Add the lemon juice to the sauce and return the chicken to the pan. Simmer gently, turning the meat occasionally, about 5 minutes or until the chicken reaches 165°F. Add the dill to the sauce and serve.

 VELOUTÉ

This sauce is based on a classic French sauce known as a velouté. It is simply a stock thickened with a roux and cooked until the flour can no longer be tasted. This simple and versatile sauce is easy to make, and its variations are only limited by your imagination.

CHICKEN AND RICOTTA POLPETTE (MEATBALLS)

INGREDIENTS

Serves 2

¾ cup plain bread crumbs

½ cup whole milk

½ pound ground chicken

4 ounces whole-milk ricotta cheese

1 large egg, beaten

¼ cup grated Parmesan cheese

2 cloves garlic, minced

4 tablespoons chopped fresh parsley

⅛ teaspoon salt

⅛ teaspoon freshly ground black pepper

Olive oil, as needed

1 (24-ounce) jar marinara sauce

1. In a medium bowl, soak the bread crumbs in the milk 10 minutes. Add all the remaining ingredients except the olive oil and marinara sauce. Mix well using your hands. Divide the mixture into eighths and roll into meatballs.

2. Heat the olive oil in a medium skillet over medium-high heat. Brown the meatballs well, about 2 minutes per side, and blot dry with paper towels.

3. Pour the marinara into a medium saucepan and add the meatballs. Simmer over medium heat 25 minutes. Serve hot.

 SELECTING MEAT FOR MEATBALLS

Most packages of ground meats today advertise the amount of fat in the meat. When making meatballs or meatloaf, it is advisable to use meat with a fat content higher than 10 percent. The finished product will be superior in flavor and texture.

PARMESAN CHICKEN

INGREDIENTS

Serves 2

2 (4-ounce) skinless, boneless
 chicken breasts, cut into
 1" pieces

2 tablespoons lemon juice

½ teaspoon sea salt

¼ teaspoon freshly ground
 black pepper

¼ teaspoon dried thyme

1 tablespoon butter

3 tablespoons grated Parmesan
 cheese

1. Sprinkle chicken pieces with lemon juice, salt, pepper, and thyme. Let stand at room temperature 10 minutes.

2. Melt butter in a heavy medium saucepan over medium heat. Add chicken and sauté until thoroughly cooked, about 5–6 minutes, stirring frequently. Sprinkle cheese over chicken, turn off heat, cover pan, and let stand 2–3 minutes to melt cheese. Serve over hot couscous if desired.

GREEK CHICKEN STIR-FRY

INGREDIENTS

Serves 2

½ pound skinless, boneless
 chicken breasts

¼ teaspoon sea salt

⅛ teaspoon freshly ground
 black pepper

1 tablespoon extra-virgin olive
 oil

1 clove garlic, minced

½ cup julienned green bell
 pepper

½ cup julienned red onion

1½ tablespoons lemon juice

¼ cup crumbled feta cheese

1. Cut chicken breasts into 1" pieces and sprinkle with salt and pepper. Heat olive oil in a wok or large skillet over medium-high heat. Add chicken and garlic and stir-fry until chicken is cooked, about 5 minutes. Remove chicken and garlic to a plate with a slotted spoon and set aside.

2. Add pepper and onion to skillet and stir-fry 5 minutes until crisp-tender. Add chicken to skillet and sprinkle with lemon juice. Stir-fry 1 minute longer. Sprinkle with feta cheese, remove pan from heat, cover, and let stand 2 minutes longer to melt cheese. Serve immediately.

 GREEK FOOD

Seasonings and ingredients that add a Greek flavor include feta cheese, oregano, olives, spinach, phyllo dough, pita bread, rice, fresh seafood, grape leaves, lamb, and yogurt.

SAUTÉED CHICKEN PATTIES

INGREDIENTS

Serves 2

2 tablespoons extra-virgin olive oil, divided

½ cup finely chopped white onion

½ teaspoon granulated sugar

1 large egg

1 cup panko, divided

¾ teaspoon sea salt, divided

⅛ teaspoon ground white pepper

½ pound ground chicken

¾ cup chicken broth

¼ teaspoon dried marjoram

1. Heat 1 tablespoon oil in a heavy medium pan over medium heat. Add onion; cook and stir 3 minutes, then sprinkle with sugar and cook, stirring occasionally, until onion begins to turn light brown, 8 minutes. Let cool.
2. Meanwhile, in a large bowl, combine egg, ½ cup panko, ½ teaspoon salt, and pepper and mix well. Add caramelized onions; do not rinse pan. Add ground chicken and mix gently but thoroughly. Form into 2 patties and coat in remaining ½ cup panko.
3. Heat remaining oil in pan used to cook onions over medium heat. Add chicken patties and sauté 4 minutes. Carefully turn patties and sauté 6 minutes longer or until thoroughly cooked. Remove to serving platter. Scrape up any dark bits of panko from the pan and discard.
4. Add chicken broth, marjoram, and remaining ¼ teaspoon salt to pan and bring to a boil over high heat. Boil 4 minutes to reduce liquid; pour over chicken patties and serve.

TERIYAKI CHICKEN

INGREDIENTS

Serves 2

½ pound skinless, boneless chicken breasts

½ cup teriyaki sauce

2 scallions, finely chopped

1 teaspoon granulated sugar

2 tablespoons minced fresh ginger

1 tablespoon vegetable or peanut oil

1 clove garlic, crushed

⅛ teaspoon red pepper flakes

1. Cut the chicken breasts into thin strips approximately 1½"–2" long. In a large bowl, combine the teriyaki sauce, scallions, sugar, and ginger. Store half the teriyaki sauce mixture in a sealed container in the refrigerator. Combine the chicken in the bowl with the remainder of the teriyaki sauce mixture and marinate in the refrigerator 30 minutes.
2. Heat a wok or skillet over medium-high heat until it is almost smoking. Add the oil. When the oil is hot, add the garlic and red pepper flakes. Stir-fry 30 seconds.
3. Add the chicken. Let brown briefly, then stir-fry, moving the chicken around the pan until it turns white and is nearly cooked, about 3–4 minutes.
4. Add the reserved marinade into the pan. Reduce the heat and cook, stirring occasionally, an additional 2 minutes or until the chicken is fully cooked and nicely glazed with the sauce. Serve hot.

BROCCOLI CHICKEN

INGREDIENTS

Serves 2

½ pound skinless, boneless chicken breasts, cut into bite-sized cubes

½ teaspoon sea salt, divided

¼ teaspoon freshly ground black pepper

½ tablespoon Chinese rice wine or dry sherry

3 cups broccoli florets

1 tablespoon oyster sauce

1½ tablespoons water

½ teaspoon brown sugar

1 cup vegetable or peanut oil

½ tablespoon minced fresh ginger

1. In a large bowl, add the chicken, ¼ teaspoon salt, pepper, and rice wine. Marinate in the refrigerator 30 minutes.

2. Chop the broccoli into bite-sized pieces. Blanch in boiling water 3 minutes or until the broccoli turns bright green. Plunge the broccoli into cold water to stop the cooking process. Drain thoroughly.

3. In a small bowl, combine the oyster sauce, water, and brown sugar. Set aside.

4. Heat a large wok or skillet over medium-high heat. Add oil. When the oil is hot, add the chicken. Stir-fry the chicken cubes until they turn white, about 1–2 minutes, using a spatula to separate the cubes. Remove from the wok and drain on a plate lined with paper towels.

5. Remove all but 1½ tablespoons oil from the wok or skillet. Reheat the oil over medium-high heat until hot, then add the minced ginger. Stir-fry 10 seconds.

6. Add the broccoli and remaining salt. Stir-fry 1 minute.

7. Add the chicken. Stir-fry the chicken 1 minute, then add the oyster sauce mixture. Cook for another minute, mixing everything together. Serve hot.

CHICKEN BREASTS WITH SPINACH AND FETA

INGREDIENTS

Serves 2

¾ cup chopped baby spinach

2 tablespoons chopped fresh chives

2 tablespoons chopped fresh dill

¼ cup crumbled feta cheese

3 tablespoons ricotta cheese

2 (6-ounce) skinless, boneless chicken breasts

¾ teaspoon sea salt

¼ teaspoon freshly ground black pepper

¼ teaspoon sweet paprika

1 tablespoon extra-virgin olive oil

1 tablespoon butter

¼ cup dry white wine

1 tablespoon minced red onions

1 clove garlic, smashed

1 tablespoon all-purpose flour

½ cup chicken stock

3 tablespoons heavy cream

1. In a medium bowl, combine spinach, chives, dill, feta, and ricotta. Set aside.

2. Using a sharp knife, cut a 3" slit into the middle of the thickest part of a chicken breast. The slit should penetrate two-thirds of the way into the chicken breast to create a pocket. Stuff half of the spinach-cheese filling into the pocket. Secure opening with toothpicks. Repeat with remaining chicken, then season with salt, pepper, and paprika.

3. Heat oil and butter in a large skillet over medium-high heat 30 seconds. Add chicken and brown 4 minutes per side. Set chicken aside and keep warm. Add wine to skillet and deglaze the pan. Cook 2 minutes or until most of the wine has evaporated. Reduce heat to medium and stir in onions, garlic, and flour. Cook 2 minutes.

4. Add stock, increase heat to medium-high, and bring sauce to a boil. Reduce heat to medium and return chicken to skillet. Cover skillet and cook 20 minutes. Remove chicken again and keep warm. Add cream and cook until sauce thickens, about 2–3 minutes.

5. Slice chicken and place on plates. Pour sauce over chicken and serve extra sauce on the side.

CHICKEN AND BLACK BEAN STEW

INGREDIENTS

Serves 2

2 chicken legs and thighs, skin on and bone in

2 tablespoons vegetable oil

1 small white onion, peeled and small diced

1 teaspoon dried oregano

½ teaspoon ground cumin

½ teaspoon chili powder

2 teaspoons tomato paste

1 (15-ounce) can black beans, undrained

½ cup chicken stock

¼ teaspoon salt

¼ teaspoon freshly ground black pepper

3 tablespoons chopped fresh cilantro

1 medium lime, cut in half

1. Using a cleaver, cut the chicken through the bones into 2" pieces. Heat the oil in a medium pot over medium-high heat. Add the chicken and brown well, about 4 minutes per side. Remove the chicken from the pot and set aside.

2. In the same pot, brown the onions over medium heat in the leftover oil, about 5–7 minutes. Add the dry spices and sauté 1 minute. Add the tomato paste and cook 1 more minute, stirring to coat the onions.

3. Add all the remaining ingredients except the cilantro and lime and simmer uncovered 30 minutes.

4. Ladle into two serving bowls. Sprinkle the cilantro on top and squeeze the lime over the stew.

LIME AND CILANTRO

Adding lime and cilantro at the end of a cooking process has a way of brightening the dish as well as giving it a distinctly Mexican flavor. Try taking some of your favorites, like chicken soup or chili or many other stews and soups, south of the border by adding these magical ingredients.

CHAPTER 9

Beef and Pork Main Dishes

SIMPLE PAN-ROASTED RIB STEAKS

INGREDIENTS
Serves 2

1 (10-ounce) package white
  mushrooms, chopped into
  pea-sized pieces

1 cup rice vinegar

1 cup granulated sugar

2 tablespoons chopped fresh
  parsley

2 (8–10-ounce) rib or
  Delmonico steaks, about 1"
  thick

⅛ teaspoon salt

⅛ teaspoon freshly ground
  black pepper

1. Combine the mushrooms, vinegar, and sugar in a medium pot and bring to a boil. Boil 5 minutes, then remove from heat and cool. Drain and toss with parsley. Refrigerate until ready to use.

2. Season the steaks well with salt and pepper. Heat a medium cast-iron skillet or a heavy pan over high heat at least 5 minutes. Add the steaks to the dry skillet. Don't turn the steaks until a few drops of juices appear on the top of the meat.

3. Turn the steaks and cook about 2 minutes for medium-rare (130°F–135°F). Let the steaks rest about 3 minutes before serving. Serve with the mushroom relish.

 BEEF COOKING TEMPERATURES
Here are some guidelines for cooking beef: rare is 120°F–125°F. Medium-rare is 130°F–135°F. Medium is 140°F–145°F. Medium-well is 150°F–155°F. Anything over 160°F is well-done.

STOVETOP LASAGNA

INGREDIENTS
Serves 2

½ pound bulk sweet Italian
  sausage

½ cup chopped white onion

4 cups cheese ravioli

1¼ cups pasta sauce

½ teaspoon dried Italian
  seasoning

¼ teaspoon sea salt

1 cup shredded Italian blend
  cheese

1. Bring a large pot of water to a boil. Meanwhile, in a medium skillet over medium heat, cook sausage and onion, stirring to break up sausage, until meat is browned, about 8–10 minutes. Drain sausage thoroughly and wipe out skillet.

2. Add ravioli to boiling water; cook until almost tender, about 1–2 minutes. Drain well. In cleaned skillet, spread about ½ cup pasta sauce, then top with layers of sausage mixture, ravioli, and more pasta sauce. Sprinkle each layer with a bit of the Italian seasoning and salt. Sprinkle final layer with cheese blend. Cover and cook over medium heat, shaking pan occasionally, until sauce bubbles, cheese melts, and mixture is hot, about 6 minutes. Serve immediately.

SEARED SKIRT STEAK WITH CILANTRO AND LIME

INGREDIENTS

Serves 2

¼ cup extra-virgin olive oil

Juice of 2 medium limes, divided

3 cloves garlic, minced

4 tablespoons chopped fresh cilantro, divided

¼ teaspoon salt, divided

¼ teaspoon freshly ground black pepper, divided

2 (8-ounce) skirt steaks

1½ cups small-diced jicama

¼ cup diced tomato

¼ cup finely minced red onion

½ medium jalapeño pepper, seeded and minced

Cooking spray

1. In a blender, combine the oil, half of the lime juice, garlic, 2 tablespoons cilantro, and ⅛ teaspoon each salt and pepper. Purée until smooth. Pour the mixture over the steaks and let marinate 1 hour in the refrigerator.

2. In a small bowl, mix together the jicama, tomato, onion, jalapeño, and the remaining lime juice and cilantro. Season with remaining salt and pepper and set aside.

3. Heat a medium pan over medium-high heat and spray with the cooking spray. Drain the steaks and wipe off most of the marinade. Add steak to the pan and sear well on both sides, about 2 minutes per side or to desired doneness. Remove from the pan and let rest 3 minutes. Serve with the salsa.

 SKIRT STEAK 101

Skirt steak is a thin muscle that acts as a diaphragm inside the cow. It is a great and often underutilized cut of beef, although it is commonly used for fajitas, a popular Southwestern dish. It is very thin and has a conspicuous grain to the meat.

RED WINE–MARINATED HANGER STEAK WITH ONIONS

INGREDIENTS

Serves 2

———

2 large white onions, peeled and thinly sliced

2 cups dry red wine

¼ cup Worcestershire sauce

3 tablespoons extra-virgin olive oil, divided

1 (1½-pound) hanger steak

¼ teaspoon salt, divided

¼ teaspoon freshly ground black pepper, divided

2 tablespoons butter

1. Mix together the onions, wine, Worcestershire sauce, and 2 tablespoons oil in a medium bowl or zip-top bag. Coat the steak in the mixture and let marinate overnight in the refrigerator.

2. Drain the marinade off the steak. Discard the liquid, but save the onions. Blot the meat dry with paper towels and season all over with half the salt and pepper.

3. Heat a medium pan over medium-high heat about 5 minutes. Rub the remaining oil over the seasoned steak and place it in the hot pan. Evenly brown all sides and cook about 2 minutes per side or to desired temperature. Remove from pan and let rest.

4. While the meat rests, melt the butter over medium heat in a small sauté pan. Sauté the marinated onions about 5 minutes. Season with remaining salt and pepper.

5. Cut the meat into slices about ½" thick. Serve the sautéed onions atop the steak.

SPICY CUBE STEAKS

INGREDIENTS

Serves 2

———

2 cube steaks

1 tablespoon all-purpose flour

½ tablespoon chili powder

½ teaspoon sea salt

1 tablespoon extra-virgin olive oil

1 cup canned diced tomatoes with green chilies

½ cup condensed nacho cheese soup

½ cup sliced mushrooms

1. Place cube steaks on waxed paper. In a small bowl, combine flour, chili powder, and salt and mix well. Sprinkle half of flour mixture over the steaks and pound into steaks using a rolling pin or the flat side of a meat mallet. Turn steaks, sprinkle with remaining flour mixture, and pound again.

2. Heat olive oil in a large saucepan over medium-high heat. Add steaks; sauté 4 minutes on first side, then turn and sauté 2 minutes. Remove steaks from saucepan. Pour tomatoes and soup into pan; cook over medium heat and stir until simmering, scraping up browned bits. Add steaks back to pan along with mushrooms; simmer 15 minutes until tender.

SLOW-COOKED BEEF BRISKET

INGREDIENTS

Serves 2

—

¼ cup peanut oil

1 (1½-pound) beef brisket, trimmed

½ cup soy sauce

2 cups chicken broth

½ cup sake

6 cloves garlic

1 (2") piece fresh gingerroot, peeled and smashed flat

1. In a heavy pot large enough to accommodate all the ingredients, heat the oil over medium-high heat until barely smoking. Add the brisket and brown well on both sides, about 5–7 minutes per side. Wipe out the excess oil from the pot and add all the remaining ingredients.
2. Bring the liquid to a boil, then reduce to a very gentle simmer. Cover the pot and simmer about 3 hours or until a knife inserted into the deepest part of the meat comes free with no resistance.

BRAISED BEEF SHORT RIBS WITH MUSHROOMS

INGREDIENTS

Serves 2

—

4 (6-ounce) short ribs, trimmed

⅛ teaspoon salt

⅛ teaspoon freshly ground black pepper

All-purpose flour, as needed

¼ cup oil

3 cups beef broth

2 cups dry red wine

1 (10-ounce) package white mushrooms, sliced

1 cup canned diced tomatoes

2 cloves garlic, minced

1. Season the ribs with salt and pepper. Dust with flour and shake off excess. Heat the oil in a medium skillet over medium-high heat and brown the ribs well on all sides, about 3–5 minutes per side.
2. Place the ribs in a medium pot along with all the remaining ingredients and bring to a boil. Immediately turn down to a simmer and cover. Cook over low heat 1½ hours or until the meat begins to fall off the bone.
3. When the meat is done, remove it from the pot. Skim off any fat and boil the liquid until about 2 cups remain. Return the meat to the sauce to warm through and serve.

 THE BASICS OF BRAISING

Braising simply means to cook slowly in liquid. Most braised items are first browned well, then placed in a flavorful liquid and cooked gently until the meat is very tender. Braising is usually reserved for tough cuts of meat that do not roast well.

TUSCAN BEEF STEW WITH SQUASH

INGREDIENTS

Serves 2

¾ pound beef stew meat, cut into 1" cubes

¾ cup all-purpose flour

⅛ teaspoon salt

⅛ teaspoon freshly ground black pepper

½ cup extra-virgin olive oil

1 small white onion, peeled and small diced

1 bulb fennel, medium diced

2 cloves garlic, minced

1 teaspoon chopped fresh rosemary

1 cup dry red wine

4 cups beef broth

1 cup cubed butternut squash (about 1" cubes)

1. Toss the meat with the flour, salt, and pepper. In a pot large enough to accommodate all of the ingredients, heat the oil over medium-high heat and brown the meat well. Remove the meat from the pot and set aside.

2. Add the onion, fennel, garlic, and rosemary to the same pot. Sauté over medium heat 4 minutes. Add the wine, stirring and scraping to loosen any cooked-on bits from the bottom of the pot.

3. Return the meat to the pot. Add the broth and bring to a boil. As soon as it boils, reduce to a gentle simmer and cook 1 hour uncovered.

4. Add the butternut squash and cook uncovered 30 minutes more or until all of the ingredients are tender. Serve hot in bowls or over pasta or bread if desired.

FLOURING MEAT FOR BROWNING

There are three reasons that meat is floured before browning. First, the flour forms an attractive crust that helps the meat to brown effectively. Second, the flour adds a toasty flavor to the dish. And third, the flour acts as a thickening agent and gives the finished sauce a nice consistency.

BEEF AND TORTELLINI

INGREDIENTS

Serves 2

½ pound ground beef

½ cup chopped white onion

2 cups beef-filled tortellini

½ cup four-cheese Alfredo sauce

5 tablespoons homemade or store-bought pesto

1. Bring a large pot of water to a boil over high heat. Meanwhile, in a large saucepan, cook ground beef and onion over medium heat 5 minutes or until beef is browned, stirring to break up meat. Drain well. Cook tortellini in boiling water according to package directions until tender; drain well.

2. Add cooked and drained tortellini and Alfredo sauce to the beef mixture and cook over medium heat 5 minutes, stirring occasionally, until mixture is combined and sauce bubbles. Stir in pesto, cover, remove from heat, let stand 5 minutes, and serve.

SAUSAGE STIR-FRY

INGREDIENTS

Serves 2

½ pound sweet Italian sausages

2 tablespoons water

1 tablespoon extra-virgin olive oil

½ cup chopped white onion

1 small yellow summer squash, sliced

½ cup broccoli florets

6 tablespoons sweet-and-sour sauce

1. In a large skillet, cook Italian sausages and water over medium heat 6 minutes, turning frequently during cooking time until water evaporates and sausages begin to brown. Remove sausages to a plate and cut into 1" pieces.

2. Drain fat from skillet but do not rinse. Return to medium-high heat, add olive oil, then add onion. Stir-fry until onion is crisp-tender, 3–4 minutes. Add squash and broccoli; stir-fry 4–5 minutes longer until broccoli is hot and squash is tender.

3. Return sausage pieces to skillet along with sweet-and-sour sauce. Stir-fry 4–6 minutes until sausage pieces are thoroughly cooked and sauce bubbles. Serve immediately.

HAM AND SWEET POTATOES

INGREDIENTS

Serves 2

½ tablespoon extra-virgin olive oil

¼ cup peeled and finely chopped yellow onion

1 (½-pound) cooked ham steak

3 tablespoons orange marmalade

1 tablespoon reserved sweet potato liquid

⅛ teaspoon ground nutmeg

½ cup canned sweet potatoes, drained, reserving 1 tablespoon liquid

⅓ cup canned mandarin oranges, drained

1. In a large skillet, heat olive oil over medium heat. Add onion; cook and stir until crisp-tender, about 3–4 minutes. Add ham to skillet along with marmalade, reserved sweet potato liquid, and nutmeg. Cover and simmer 10 minutes over medium-low heat.

2. Turn ham steak, then add sweet potatoes to skillet; cover and simmer 5 minutes. Stir in mandarin oranges; cover and cook 2–4 minutes longer until hot. Serve immediately.

SKILLET PORK CHOPS WITH CABBAGE

INGREDIENTS

Serves 2

1½ tablespoons extra-virgin
    olive oil

½ cup chopped red onion

2 (4-ounce) smoked pork chops

1½ cups shredded red cabbage

½ cup peeled and chopped
    Granny Smith apple

½ cup apple juice

¼ teaspoon dried thyme

¼ teaspoon sea salt

⅛ teaspoon freshly ground
    black pepper

1. Heat olive oil in a large skillet over medium heat. Add onion; cook and stir 3–4 minutes until crisp-tender. Add pork chops; brown on both sides about 3 minutes. Add cabbage and apple to the skillet; cook and stir 3 minutes.

2. Pour apple juice over all and sprinkle with thyme, salt, and pepper. Bring to a boil, then reduce heat to medium, cover, and simmer 10 minutes until cabbage is crisp-tender and pork chops are hot and tender. Serve immediately.

CUBAN PORK CHOPS

INGREDIENTS

Serves 2

2 (4-ounce) boneless pork loin
    chops

2 cloves garlic, finely chopped

1 teaspoon ground cumin

¼ teaspoon dried oregano

½ teaspoon sea salt

⅛ teaspoon cayenne pepper

1 tablespoon extra-virgin olive
    oil

2 tablespoons orange juice

1½ tablespoons lime juice

1. Trim excess fat from pork chops. In a small bowl, combine garlic, cumin, oregano, salt, and cayenne pepper and mix well. Sprinkle this mixture on both sides of chops and rub into meat. Let stand at room temperature 10 minutes.

2. Heat olive oil in a heavy saucepan over medium heat. Add pork chops and cook 5 minutes. Carefully turn and cook 5 minutes on second side. Add orange juice and lime juice and bring to a simmer.

3. Cover pan and simmer chops 5–10 minutes or until pork chops are tender and just slightly pink in the center and sauce is reduced. Serve immediately.

SLOW-COOKED THAI LONG BEANS WITH PORK

INGREDIENTS

Serves 2

¼ cup peanut oil

½ pound ground pork

6 cloves garlic, minced

2 Thai chili peppers (bird peppers) or 2 small jalapeño peppers, minced

1 pound Chinese long beans, cut into 4" pieces

2 cups chicken broth

3 tablespoons Thai fish sauce

¼ cup soy sauce

1 tablespoon granulated sugar

1. Heat the oil in a wok or heavy pan over high heat until barely smoking. Add the pork and brown well.
2. Add the garlic and peppers and cook 2 minutes.
3. Add all the remaining ingredients. Cover and simmer gently 15 minutes. Serve hot as is or over rice if desired.

THAI FISH SAUCE

Fish sauce is potent! It smells awful straight from the bottle, with a scent resembling that of old socks. But used properly, it lends a complex saltiness that adds much to the dishes it seasons.

BEEF STIR-FRY

INGREDIENTS

Serves 2

½ pound sirloin steak

¼ cup plus 1 tablespoon stir-fry sauce, divided

1 tablespoon vegetable or peanut oil

½ cup chopped white onion

¾ cup sugar snap peas

½ small red bell pepper, seeded and thinly sliced

1. Thinly slice the steak across the grain. Place in a medium bowl and toss with 1 tablespoon stir-fry sauce. Set aside.
2. Heat oil in a large skillet or wok over medium-high heat. Add onion; stir-fry 3–4 minutes until crisp-tender. Add peas and bell pepper; stir-fry 2–3 minutes. Add beef; stir-fry 3–4 minutes until browned. Add remaining ¼ cup stir-fry sauce and bring to a simmer; simmer 3–4 minutes until blended. Serve alone or over hot cooked rice if desired.

STIR-FRY VARIATIONS

Once you've learned a stir-fry recipe, you can vary it with many different cuts of meat and lots of vegetables. Just be sure that the veggies are cut to about the same size so they cook in the same amount of time. And experiment with different bottled stir-fry sauces you'll find in the Asian aisle of your supermarket.

CHAPTER 10

Fish and Seafood Main Dishes

MONKFISH MEDALLIONS WITH PROVENÇAL SALSA

INGREDIENTS

Serves 2

---

1 cup diced tomato

¼ cup finely minced red onion

2 tablespoons chopped and pitted niçoise olives

1 tablespoon capers, rinsed

1 clove garlic, minced

2 tablespoons chopped fresh basil

4 tablespoons extra-virgin olive oil, divided

¼ teaspoon salt, divided

¼ teaspoon freshly ground black pepper, divided

1 teaspoon fresh thyme

1 (12–16-ounce) monkfish fillet, cut into 6 medallions

1. To make the salsa, combine the tomatoes, onion, olives, capers, garlic, basil, 2 tablespoons olive oil, and half of the salt and pepper in a medium bowl. Set aside.
2. Toss the monkfish medallions with the remaining olive oil, the thyme, and the remaining salt and pepper. Heat a medium nonstick pan over medium heat, add the fish, and sauté about 2 minutes per side or until piping hot in the center.
3. Mound the salsa in the center of two serving plates and arrange 3 fish medallions around the salsa on each plate.

 THE FLAVORS OF PROVENCE
Provence is a region in France famous for its tomatoes, garlic, olive oil, and olives. The climate and agriculture provide France with superior produce and a cuisine unique to the area.

HOISIN-GLAZED SHRIMP

INGREDIENTS

Serves 2

---

2 tablespoons peanut oil

1 pound raw jumbo shrimp, peeled and deveined

1 teaspoon chopped fresh ginger

1 tablespoon soy sauce

Juice of 1 medium lemon

1 tablespoon hoisin sauce

1. In a medium heavy sauté pan or wok, heat the oil over medium-high heat until barely smoking. Add the shrimp and ginger and sauté about 2 minutes.
2. Add the soy sauce and lemon juice and cook 1 minute.
3. Add the hoisin and sauté 1 more minute or until the shrimp are well coated and fully cooked. Serve hot over rice if desired.

SWORDFISH WITH ANCHOVY AND CAPER SAUCE

INGREDIENTS

Serves 2

2 tablespoons extra-virgin
olive oil

2 (8-ounce) swordfish fillets

⅛ teaspoon salt

⅛ teaspoon freshly ground
black pepper

2 tablespoons butter

2 anchovy fillets, chopped

Juice of 1 medium lemon

2 tablespoons capers, rinsed

2 tablespoons chopped fresh
parsley

1. Heat a medium skillet over medium-high heat. Add the olive oil and heat until barely smoking.
2. Season the swordfish on both sides with salt and pepper and brown well on both sides, about 4–5 minutes per side, making sure that the center of the fish is hot. Transfer the fish to a plate and keep warm.
3. Wipe out the pan and return to medium-high heat. Add the butter and anchovies to the pan and heat until the butter begins to turn slightly brown. Immediately add the lemon juice, capers, and parsley. Turn off the heat and stir the sauce to mix.
4. Pour the sauce over the fish and serve.

 THE ECOLOGY OF EATING

It is important to remember that large pelagic fish, such as swordfish and tuna, are a natural resource that can easily be depleted. Limit your consumption of these giants to a few times a year to help ensure the species' survival.

POACHED GROUPER FILLETS

INGREDIENTS

Serves 2

2 (8-ounce) skinless grouper
fillets

½ cup vermouth

¼ cup chicken stock

2 tablespoons minced shallots

1 tablespoon butter

⅛ teaspoon salt

⅛ teaspoon freshly ground
black pepper

2 teaspoons chopped fresh dill

1. Place the fish, vermouth, chicken stock, shallots, butter, salt, and pepper in a shallow pan.
2. Bring the liquid to a boil, then reduce heat to the lowest setting. Cover the pan and cook about 6 minutes or until the centers of the fillets are hot.
3. Transfer the fish to shallow bowls. Add the dill to the sauce in the pan, then pour the sauce over the fish. Serve with a lot of sauce, with a spoon to eat it like soup.

CRISPY AND RARE TUNA SLABS

INGREDIENTS

Serves 2

2 medium cucumbers, thinly
sliced

2 tablespoons rice vinegar

2 tablespoons granulated sugar

1 (12–16-ounce) slab tuna

2 tablespoons soy sauce

2 tablespoons peanut oil or
vegetable oil

1. Toss the cucumbers in a small bowl with the vinegar and sugar, let marinate 30 minutes, then drain.
2. Place the tuna and soy sauce in a medium bowl and marinate 15 minutes, then blot dry.
3. Heat the oil in a medium pan over medium-high heat until barely smoking. Sear the tuna quickly on all sides, no more than 20–30 seconds per side. Remove from the pan.
4. To serve, place a pile of the cucumbers in the center of each plate. Slice the tuna into slabs about ½" thick and arrange around the cucumbers. You can also serve this dish with wasabi and ginger as a sashimi course.

SAUTÉED MAKO SHARK STEAKS

INGREDIENTS

Serves 2

2 (6–8-ounce) mako shark fillets, about 1" thick

⅛ teaspoon salt

⅛ teaspoon freshly ground
black pepper

½ cup all-purpose flour

2 tablespoons butter, divided

2 tablespoons extra-virgin
olive oil, divided

1 (10-ounce) package white
mushrooms, thinly sliced

Juice of 1 medium lemon

2 tablespoons chopped fresh
chives

1. Season each piece of fish with salt and pepper and dust with flour. Be sure to shake off any excess flour.
2. Preheat a medium heavy skillet over medium heat and add 1 tablespoon butter and 1 tablespoon oil. Heat until the butter stops bubbling, add the fish, and sauté about 5 minutes per side. The outside should be golden brown and the center piping hot. Remove the fish from the pan and keep warm.
3. Wipe out the pan and add the remaining butter and oil. Heat over medium-high heat until the butter stops bubbling. Add the mushrooms and sauté until all of the water they release has evaporated, about 4 minutes. Add the lemon juice and cook 1 minute. Add the chives and adjust seasoning with additional salt and pepper if needed. Serve the mushrooms on top of the mako steaks.

CURRY AND COCONUT STEAMED MUSSELS

INGREDIENTS

Serves 2

———

2 tablespoons vegetable oil

1 small white onion, peeled and minced

2 tablespoons curry powder

3 pounds mussels, washed and picked over

1 cup coconut milk

1 cup dry white wine

½ cup shredded fresh basil

1. Heat the oil over medium-high heat in a pot large enough to accommodate all of the mussels when they open. Add the onion and curry and sauté about 2 minutes.
2. Add the mussels, coconut milk, and wine. Cover and cook over high heat until the mussels open, about 4 minutes.
3. Turn off the heat and add the basil. Toss to mix. Serve in large bowls as is or with bread to soak up the broth.

 CHOOSING MUSSELS

Mussels, like all shellfish, should be closed or close when they are tapped. They should be heavy for their size and smell like the sea. They also should have a federal shellfish tag attached to them that tells the consumer when the shellfish was harvested. Ask your fishmonger to show you this tag, and do not choose shellfish that have been out of the water for more than four days.

OYSTER "PAN ROAST"

INGREDIENTS

Serves 2

———

2 cups half-and-half

2 cups clam juice

2 tablespoons Worcestershire sauce

Dash Tabasco sauce

⅛ teaspoon salt

⅛ teaspoon freshly ground black pepper

12 shucked oysters, with their liquid

2 tablespoons butter

4 tablespoons chopped fresh chives

In a small pot, combine the half-and-half, clam juice, Worcestershire sauce, Tabasco, salt, and pepper; bring to a boil. As soon as the mixture boils, turn off the heat and add the oysters and the butter. Stir until the butter is melted. Divide between two bowls, top with chives, and serve.

 IN MODERATION

This is a very rich dish, suffused with cream and butter. It should be enjoyed as an occasional treat, perhaps during the winter holidays or on New Year's Eve. You can vary the dish with almost any shellfish you like. It is excellent with clams and mussels.

STIR-FRIED BLACKFISH WITH BLACK BEAN SAUCE

INGREDIENTS

Serves 2

3 tablespoons peanut oil

1 cup sliced shiitake
    mushrooms

½ cup julienned red bell pepper

3 scallions, thinly sliced

2 cloves garlic, minced

2 teaspoons grated fresh
    ginger

1 (12-ounce) skinless blackfish
    fillet, cut into 2" chunks

½ cup chicken stock or water

2 tablespoons soy sauce

1 tablespoon prepared Chinese
    black bean sauce

Pinch granulated sugar

2 tablespoons cornstarch dis-
    solved in 2 tablespoons cold
    water

1. In a large pan or wok, heat the peanut oil over high heat until smoking.
2. Add the mushrooms, bell pepper, scallions, garlic, and ginger. Stir-fry about 2 minutes. Add the fish and cook another 2 minutes.
3. Add the stock, soy sauce, black bean sauce, and sugar. Bring to a boil and let boil 2 minutes.
4. With the sauce still boiling, slowly drizzle in the cornstarch slurry, stirring the sauce constantly. Turn off the heat immediately and serve.

 BLACK BEAN SAUCE

This interesting ingredient can be found in almost any supermarket these days. It is a mixture of small fermented black beans, soy, and seasonings. A little goes a long way, so experiment with how much you like.

TWO-HOUR CALAMARI STEW WITH SPINACH

INGREDIENTS

Serves 2

1 small red onion, peeled and
   roughly chopped

1 medium carrot, peeled and
   roughly chopped

1 stalk celery, roughly chopped

4 cloves garlic, peeled

¼ cup chopped fresh parsley

½ cup extra-virgin olive oil

1 pound cleaned calamari, cut
   into rings, legs cut in half

½ cup dry red wine

1 (24-ounce) jar marinara
   sauce

Pinch red pepper flakes

1 (10-ounce) package curly
   spinach, stems removed and
   roughly chopped

⅛ teaspoon salt

⅛ teaspoon freshly ground
   black pepper

1. Place the onion, carrot, celery, garlic, parsley, and olive oil in a food processor. Pulse until the mixture is the texture of pickle relish.

2. Transfer the vegetable mixture to a medium saucepot and cook over medium heat, stirring frequently until it becomes golden in color, about 10 minutes.

3. Add the calamari and wine, increase heat and boil about 2 minutes. Add the marinara and red pepper flakes. Reduce heat to low and simmer gently 1½ hours partially covered.

4. Add the spinach and simmer partially covered 30 minutes. Season with salt and pepper and serve in a bowl or over pasta.

 SOFRITO

This mixture of ground veggies cooked in olive oil is known as a sofrito. Many Latin cultures have sofritos of some kind. Sometimes the vegetables and spices are cooked, and sometimes they're puréed raw. But they always play the same role of adding a lot of flavor.

SCALLOP AND CORN SAUTÉ

INGREDIENTS

Serves 2

---

2 tablespoons peanut oil

¾ pound sea scallops, patted dry

¼ teaspoon salt, divided

¼ teaspoon freshly ground black pepper, divided

10 white mushrooms, sliced

2 ears fresh corn, kernels cut from the cob

1 tablespoon butter

2 tablespoons chopped fresh chives

1 tablespoon truffle oil

1. In a large skillet, heat the peanut oil over medium-high heat until barely smoking. Season the scallops with half of the salt and pepper and add them to the pan in a single layer. Do not crowd the pan. Cook on one side until browned, about 2 minutes.
2. Add the mushrooms and the corn kernels and stir well. Cook about 3 minutes or until the mushrooms begin to release their juices and the corn starts to become tender.
3. Add the butter, chives, and truffle oil. Turn off heat and stir to mix. Season with remaining salt and pepper and serve.

 AREN'T TRUFFLES CHOCOLATE?

Truffles are a member of the mushroom family and grow primarily in France and Italy. The Italian white truffle is far more fragrant than the French black truffle. Look for white truffle oil in specialty markets. Refrigerate unused oil for up to a year.

SHRIMP IN PESTO CREAM

INGREDIENTS

Serves 2

---

1 pound raw medium shrimp, peeled and deveined

¾ cup heavy whipping cream

¼ cup prepared pesto

⅛ teaspoon salt

⅛ teaspoon freshly ground black pepper

Combine all the ingredients in a medium sauté pan and boil fairly hard about 5 minutes or until the shrimp turn pink and the sauce thickens. Serve immediately.

 BEWARE THE PINE NUTS!

It is important to remember that pesto almost always contains pine nuts, and that people with nut allergies may have an adverse reaction. Although most people with food allergies are quite vocal about their special needs, they sometimes forget or overlook them, especially after a few glasses of wine. Always announce the presence of nuts or nut oils when serving a dish to avoid any unpleasant accidents.

GARLICKY SHRIMP SAUTÉ

INGREDIENTS

Serves 2

2 tablespoons extra-virgin olive oil

2 ounces chorizo, finely chopped

1 small white onion, peeled and finely chopped

2 cloves garlic, minced

¾ pound raw medium shrimp, peeled and deveined

1 (15-ounce) can butter beans, drained and rinsed

1 medium plum tomato, chopped

¼ cup dry white wine

1 tablespoon butter

1 teaspoon fresh thyme

⅛ teaspoon salt

⅛ teaspoon freshly ground black pepper

1. Heat the olive oil in a large skillet over medium-high heat until barely smoking. Add the chorizo, onions, and garlic. Sauté about 3 minutes or until the onions are golden.
2. Add the shrimp and sauté 1 minute.
3. Add the butter beans, tomato, and wine and cook 2 minutes.
4. Add the butter, thyme, salt, and pepper. Turn off heat and stir until the butter is melted. Serve immediately.

 MMMMMM PORK

A little bit of smoked pork product goes a long way. In Italy, Spain, and many other countries, a small amount of bacon or smoked sausage is often added to fish and vegetable dishes to enhance flavors. Americans carried this over mostly in the South, but it's also done in the true chowders of the Northeast.

PAN-ROASTED SEA SCALLOPS

INGREDIENTS

Serves 2

2 tablespoons butter

1 tablespoon extra-virgin olive oil

¾ pound sea scallops, patted dry

¼ teaspoon salt, divided

¼ teaspoon freshly ground black pepper, divided

½ pound oyster mushrooms, trimmed of hard stems and torn into ½" strips

2 teaspoons fresh thyme (or ½ teaspoon dried)

3 tablespoons dry white wine

1. Heat the butter and oil in a large skillet over medium-high heat until the butter stops bubbling. Season the scallops with half of the salt and pepper. Lay them in the pan in a single layer with some room between each scallop. Increase heat to high, and don't move the scallops. Allow them to brown well on one side, about 2 minutes.

2. Turn the scallops over and add the mushrooms and thyme to the pan. Stir to coat the mushrooms with the butter. Cook over high heat until the water that releases from the mushrooms evaporates, about 5–8 minutes.

3. Add the wine and cook about 1 minute or until evaporated. Season with remaining salt and pepper and serve immediately.

 BUBBLING BUTTER

The reason that the butter should be heated until it stops bubbling is simple. The bubbling is the water that is in the butter boiling away. In order for the butter to achieve maximum temperature, the water must evaporate.

BOILED BLUE CRABS OVER NEWSPAPER

INGREDIENTS

Serves 2

1 small white onion, peeled and cut in half

3 tablespoons Old Bay Seasoning

2 medium lemons, cut in half

6 cloves garlic

4 bay leaves

1 gallon water

6 tablespoons salt

2 (12-ounce) bottles of beer

8 live blue crabs

1 newspaper, day unimportant

1. Place everything except the crabs and the newspaper in a large pot and boil 10 minutes.

2. Add the crabs to the pot and turn off heat. Cover and let poach 5 minutes.

3. Spread the newspaper out on a table. Place the crabs directly on the newspaper. Crack the crabs with mallets and eat, and serve additional beer to drink.

CHAPTER 11

Vegetarian Main Dishes

BABY VEGETABLE FRICASSEE

INGREDIENTS

Serves 2

---

2 tablespoons butter

½ cup peeled baby carrots

6 medium baby pattypan
   squash, cut in half

1 cup small white mushrooms

1 cup peeled pearl onions

1 cup baby turnips, cut in half,
   greens removed

1 cup vegetable stock

1 tablespoon chopped fresh
   rosemary

⅛ teaspoon salt

⅛ teaspoon freshly ground
   black pepper

¼ cup dry red wine

1. Melt the butter in a large pan over medium-high heat. Add all of the vegetables and cook until the mushrooms release their juices and the juices evaporate, about 5–8 minutes.
2. Add the vegetable stock and rosemary and cover the pan. Reduce the heat to low and cook about 7 minutes.
3. Remove the lid and season with salt and pepper. Increase the heat to high and cook until the stock has totally evaporated. Add the wine and continue to cook until the wine has evaporated and the vegetables are glazed, stirring throughout. Serve hot.

YUCA CON MOJO

INGREDIENTS

Serves 2

½ pound peeled yuca, cut into
   1½" chunks

½ teaspoon sea salt, divided

1½ tablespoons fresh-squeezed
   lime juice, divided

2 tablespoons extra-virgin
   olive oil

2 cloves garlic, finely chopped

2 teaspoons chopped fresh
   herb, such as cilantro or
   parsley

1. Add the yuca, ¼ teaspoon salt, ½ teaspoon lime juice, and enough water to cover to a large pot; cover and bring to a simmer over medium heat. Simmer 20 minutes; yuca should be fork-tender, but not mushy. Drain; remove woody center core. Transfer to a plate and cover to keep warm.
2. In a small skillet, heat the oil over medium heat. Remove pan from heat and add the garlic. Stir in herbs, remaining salt, and remaining lime juice. Pour this sauce over the yuca and serve immediately.

MIXED MUSHROOM STEW

INGREDIENTS

Serves 2

3 tablespoons butter

1 cup peeled pearl onions

2 stalks celery, cut into ¼"
slices

1 medium carrot, peeled and
cut into ¼" slices

1 bay leaf

3 tablespoons all-purpose flour

1 tablespoon tomato paste

½ pound white mushrooms,
quartered

½ pound oyster mushrooms,
trimmed and torn

½ pound shiitake mushrooms,
stems removed and cut in
half

½ cup dry red wine

3 cups vegetable stock

¼ teaspoon salt

¼ teaspoon freshly ground
black pepper

1 medium Idaho potato, peeled
and cut into ½" cubes

1. In a medium pot, heat the butter over medium heat until it stops bubbling. Add the pearl onions, celery, carrot, and bay leaf. Sauté until the onions are golden brown, about 8 minutes. Add the flour and stir well.

2. Add the tomato paste and cook 1 minute. Add all the mushrooms and cook about 5 minutes or until the mushrooms have released a fair amount of liquid.

3. Add the wine, stock, salt, and pepper. Simmer gently about 20 minutes uncovered.

4. Add the potatoes, reduce heat to low, and cook 15 more minutes uncovered. Adjust seasoning with additional salt and pepper if needed and serve.

 MUSHROOMS

If you can't find these specific mushrooms, don't let it stop you from making this dish. Look for any mushrooms that you can find. Experiment with different mushrooms, such as cremini, porcini, hen of the woods, morels, and chanterelles; they will all make an excellent stew.

VEGETARIAN CURRY STIR-FRY

INGREDIENTS

Serves 2

1 tablespoon extra-virgin olive oil

½ small yellow onion, peeled and sliced

1 small green bell pepper, seeded and sliced

1 teaspoon curry powder

1½ tablespoons all-purpose flour

¼ teaspoon sea salt

⅛ teaspoon red pepper flakes

½ pound firm tofu, cubed

¾ cup coconut milk

1. In a medium saucepan over medium-high heat, combine olive oil, onion, and peppers and cook 4–5 minutes, stirring frequently, until crisp-tender.
2. In a small bowl, combine curry powder, flour, salt, and red pepper flakes. Sprinkle over onion mixture. Cook and stir 3–4 minutes until bubbly.
3. Add tofu and coconut milk to the saucepan. Reduce heat to medium and cook, stirring occasionally, 5–8 minutes until sauce is thickened and tofu is hot. Serve immediately.

ABOUT TOFU

There are two different types of tofu available in the supermarket: regular and silken. Regular tofu is firmer than silken tofu. Firm or extra-firm regular tofu can be sliced or cut into cubes; it's perfect for stir-fries and grilling. Silken tofu is usually used for dressings or puddings.

VEGGIE BURRITOS

INGREDIENTS

Serves 2

1 tablespoon extra-virgin olive oil

½ cup chopped red onion

¼ teaspoon red pepper flakes

1 cup broccoli and cauliflower florets

¾ cup canned black beans, drained and rinsed

2 (10") flour tortillas

¾ cup shredded pepper jack cheese

1. Heat a large skillet over medium heat. Add olive oil and onion; cook and stir 3–4 minutes until crisp-tender. Sprinkle with red pepper flakes; cook and stir 1 minute.
2. Add broccoli and cauliflower; cook and stir 3–5 minutes until hot. Stir in black beans, cover, and let simmer 3–4 minutes.
3. Meanwhile, warm tortillas in a stainless steel skillet over medium heat about 30 seconds each side. Spread tortillas on work surface, divide vegetable mixture between them, sprinkle with cheese, and roll up, folding in sides. Serve immediately.

AVOCADO SASHIMI WITH MISO DRESSING

INGREDIENTS

Serves 2

1 medium ripe Hass avocado, halved, pitted, and peeled

1 medium lemon

1 teaspoon white or yellow miso paste

1 teaspoon grated fresh ginger

1 teaspoon light soy sauce

1 teaspoon granulated sugar

1 teaspoon sesame oil

Wasabi paste, for garnish

Pickled ginger, for garnish

1. Place the avocado halves cut-side down on a board; score them at ⅛" intervals, leaving the stem end connected to hold them together. Squeeze the lemon over the scored avocados to prevent browning. Fan the avocados onto two small plates.

2. In a small bowl, whisk together the miso paste, ginger, soy sauce, sugar, and sesame oil until the sugar is dissolved. Spoon some of the dressing over the avocados. Serve garnished with wasabi and pickled ginger.

POTATO CURRY

INGREDIENTS

Serves 2

2½ cups packaged refrigerated hash brown potatoes

1½ tablespoons extra-virgin olive oil

½ cup chopped white onion

2 cloves garlic, minced

1 tablespoon curry powder

½ teaspoon sea salt

⅛ teaspoon red pepper flakes

1 cup baby green peas

½ cup sour cream

1. Drain potatoes well, if necessary. Spread on paper towels to dry. Meanwhile, in a large skillet, heat olive oil over medium heat. Add onion and garlic; cook and stir 3–4 minutes until crisp-tender. Sprinkle curry powder, salt, and red pepper flakes into skillet; cook and stir 1 minute longer.

2. Add potatoes to skillet; cook and stir 8 minutes until potatoes are hot and tender and browning around the edges. Stir in peas and cook 2–3 minutes longer.

3. Remove from heat and stir in sour cream. Cover and let stand 3 minutes, then serve immediately.

HONEY-ORANGE BEETS

INGREDIENTS

Serves 2

---

3 medium fresh beets

½ teaspoon grated orange zest

1 tablespoon orange juice

1 teaspoon butter

½ teaspoon honey

⅛ teaspoon ground ginger

¼ teaspoon sea salt

⅛ teaspoon freshly ground
black pepper

1. Boil beets in enough water to cover 30 minutes or until fork-tender. Drain beets and let cool slightly. Slip off skins and slice.
2. In a small saucepan, heat the orange zest, orange juice, butter, honey, ginger, salt, and pepper over low heat until the butter melts. Add the beets and toss to coat.

HERB-MIXED TURNIPS

INGREDIENTS

Serves 2

---

1 pound turnips and rutabagas, peeled

1 tablespoon butter

½ tablespoon chopped fresh
parsley

1 teaspoon chopped fresh
chervil or tarragon

1 tablespoon chopped fresh
chives

1 clove garlic, finely chopped

¼ teaspoon kosher salt

⅛ teaspoon freshly ground
black pepper

¼ cup fresh bread crumbs
browned in ½ tablespoon
olive oil or butter

1. Cook the turnips and rutabagas separately in salted water until they're al dente (tender but firm—approximately 10 minutes for turnips, 20 minutes for rutabagas); drain. Carefully chop into 1"–2" pieces.
2. In a large skillet over medium heat, melt the butter. Add the turnips and rutabagas, increase the heat to medium-high, and cook until golden brown, about 5–7 minutes. Add herbs, garlic, salt, and pepper and toss to coat. Serve topped with bread crumbs.

STIR-FRIED ASIAN GREENS

INGREDIENTS

Serves 2

---

1 cup thinly sliced collard
greens

1 cup thinly sliced Chinese
cabbage (barrel-shaped napa
cabbage)

1 cup watercress leaves, stem
ends trimmed

1 tablespoon peanut oil

4 large white or cremini mushrooms, sliced

1 medium carrot, peeled and
julienned

¼ cup snow peas, halved
diagonally

¼ cup sliced red onion (first
halved, then sliced with
the grain)

1 (1") piece fresh gingerroot,
peeled and julienned

2 cloves garlic, finely chopped

¼ teaspoon sea salt

⅛ teaspoon ground white
pepper

½ tablespoon soy sauce

¼ tablespoon Chinese cooking
wine or dry sherry

¼ teaspoon toasted sesame oil

Black sesame seeds or toasted
white sesame seeds, for garnish (optional)

1. Mix together the collards, cabbage, and watercress; wash thoroughly and dry.

2. Heat the peanut oil in a large skillet over high heat until it is
shimmery, but not smoky. Add the mushrooms, carrots, snow
peas, onion, ginger, and garlic; sauté 2 minutes, stirring frequently and allowing some parts to brown. Season it well with
salt and white pepper.

3. Add the greens, soy sauce, wine, and sesame oil. Toss or stir; cook
only 1–2 minutes until the greens begin to wilt. Sprinkle with
sesame seeds and serve immediately as is or over jasmine rice.

SZECHUAN STIR-FRIED CABBAGE WITH HOT PEPPERS

INGREDIENTS

Serves 2

3 tablespoons peanut or other neutral oil, divided

4 dried red chili peppers, quartered and seeded

1 (1") piece fresh gingerroot, peeled and finely chopped

½ medium head cabbage (preferably Chinese cabbage, but any variety is okay), washed and chopped into 2" pieces

¼ teaspoon cornstarch

½ tablespoon soy sauce

½ teaspoon dry sherry or Chinese cooking wine

½ teaspoon granulated sugar

½ teaspoon rice wine vinegar

½ teaspoon toasted sesame oil

1. Heat 2 tablespoons oil in a wok or medium skillet over high heat. Add the peppers and fry, stirring, 1 minute or until the peppers darken in color. Transfer the peppers and oil to a bowl and set aside.

2. Pour remaining 1 tablespoon oil into the wok; add the ginger and cook a few seconds until fragrant. Add the cabbage all at once. Fry, stirring, 1 minute.

3. Combine the cornstarch, soy sauce, and sherry together in a small bowl. Add to the wok. Stir until the cornstarch cooks and forms a thick sauce.

4. Add the sugar and vinegar. Sprinkle in the sesame oil and pour in the red peppers and their oil. Stir to combine well. Transfer to a serving bowl and serve immediately.

SPICY VEGETARIAN CHILI

INGREDIENTS

Serves 2

1 (15-ounce) can spicy chili beans, undrained

1 cup canned diced tomatoes with green chilies, undrained

½ cup tomato salsa

½ tablespoon chili powder

½ small green bell pepper, seeded and chopped

½ cup water

In a large saucepan, combine all ingredients. Bring to a boil, then reduce heat and simmer 15 minutes, stirring occasionally, until peppers are crisp-tender and mixture is heated and blended. Serve immediately topped with sour cream, grated cheese, and chopped green onions if desired.

SWISS CHARD ROLLS WITH ROOT VEGETABLES

INGREDIENTS

Serves 2

4 large Swiss chard leaves, thoroughly washed

1½ tablespoons extra-virgin olive oil, divided

1 cup roughly chopped red onion

1 medium carrot, peeled and roughly chopped

1 medium sweet potato (about ¼ pound), peeled and finely diced

4 cups diced root vegetables (such as celery root, parsnips, turnips, and white potatoes)

2 tablespoons roughly chopped fresh Italian parsley

Juice of 1 medium lime (about 2 tablespoons)

1 teaspoon chopped fresh cilantro

¼ teaspoon kosher salt, plus more for water

⅛ teaspoon freshly ground black pepper

½ cup vegetable stock

1. Remove the stems from the chard; chop them finely.
2. Heat 1 tablespoon olive oil over medium heat in a heavy-bottomed Dutch oven or large skillet. Add the chard stems, red onion, carrots, sweet potatoes, root vegetables, parsley, lime juice, cilantro, salt, and pepper. Cook, stirring occasionally, until the root vegetables are fork-tender, about 5–8 minutes.
3. Meanwhile, bring a large pot of salted water to a boil. Blanch the chard leaves 3–4 minutes, then drain and cool.
4. Spoon ¼ cup of filling onto the stem end of a chard leaf. Fold in the sides to envelop the filling; roll away from yourself, keeping even tension so the rolls remain plump.
5. Use the remaining olive oil to grease a medium skillet. Line up the rolls in the skillet; add stock. Cook 10 minutes over medium heat; serve garnished with remaining filling.

MUSHROOM RISOTTO

INGREDIENTS

Serves 2

---

2 cups vegetable stock

1½ tablespoons extra-virgin
   olive oil

¾ cup diced assorted fresh
   mushrooms

¼ teaspoon dried thyme

½ cup Arborio rice

½ cup grated Parmesan cheese

⅛ teaspoon freshly ground
   black pepper

1 tablespoon butter

1. Heat vegetable stock in a small saucepan over low heat. Let sit over low heat while you make the risotto.
2. Place olive oil in a large saucepan over medium heat. When hot, add the mushrooms and thyme. Cook and stir until mushrooms give up their liquid and the liquid evaporates, about 6–8 minutes. Stir in rice; cook and stir 3–4 minutes until rice is opaque.
3. Add ¼ cup of the stock to the rice mixture; cook and stir until liquid is absorbed. Continue to add stock ¼ cup at a time, stirring frequently, until rice is tender and mixture is creamy.
4. When all the stock is added and rice is tender, remove from the heat and stir in cheese, pepper, and butter; cover and let stand 5 minutes. Stir and serve immediately.

ARTICHOKE STIR-FRY

INGREDIENTS

Serves 2

---

1 cup canned artichoke hearts,
   drained, reserving 2 tablespoons liquid

2 tablespoons extra-virgin
   olive oil

1 cup sliced cremini mushrooms

2 cloves garlic, minced

¼ teaspoon sea salt

⅛ teaspoon freshly ground
   black pepper

¼ teaspoon dried thyme

1 cup canned cannellini beans,
   drained and rinsed

2 tablespoons grated Romano
   cheese

1. Cut artichoke hearts into thirds and set aside. In a large skillet, heat olive oil over medium heat. Add mushrooms; cook and stir 4–5 minutes until tender. Sprinkle with garlic, salt, pepper, and thyme; cook and stir 1 minute longer.
2. Add drained artichoke hearts and cannellini beans along with reserved artichoke liquid. Cook and stir 4–5 minutes until ingredients are hot. Sprinkle with cheese, cover pan, remove from heat, and let stand 4 minutes. Stir and serve immediately.

 COMPLETE PROTEINS

When planning vegetarian menus, it's important to consider complete proteins. Your body needs complete proteins to heal injuries and keep healthy. Beans and grains are a common combination that provides these proteins. You don't need to fulfill all the requirements in one day; balancing over a two-day period is just fine.

CHAPTER 12

Pasta, Beans, and Rice

ORECCHIETTE WITH CHICKEN SAUSAGE AND BROCCOLI

INGREDIENTS

Serves 2

¼ cup extra-virgin olive oil, divided

½ pound chicken sausage, cut into 1" pieces

3 cloves garlic, minced

Pinch red pepper flakes

1 small roasted red pepper, cut into 1" strips

½ pound orecchiette pasta

2 cups broccoli florets

⅛ teaspoon salt

⅛ teaspoon freshly ground black pepper

1 cup grated Romano cheese

1. Heat a pot of water for the pasta.
2. In a large sauté pan, heat half of the oil over medium heat until barely smoking and brown the sausage very well, about 8 minutes. Add the garlic and red pepper flakes. Cook until the garlic is golden and fragrant, about 1 minute. Add the roasted red pepper and remove the pan from the heat.
3. Drop the pasta in the water and begin cooking it according to package directions. Exactly halfway through the cooking process, add the broccoli to the pot. (This eliminates the step of cooking the broccoli separately.) When the pasta is cooked, the broccoli will be perfect.
4. Return the pan with the sausage to medium heat and bring up to temperature. Drain the pasta/broccoli and add to the pan. Add the remaining olive oil and season with salt and pepper. Divide into two bowls and serve the cheese at the table to be sprinkled on top.

FRAGRANT BASIL PASTA

INGREDIENTS

Serves 2

½ pound long pasta

½ cup extra-virgin olive oil

6 cloves garlic, thinly sliced

2 cups chiffonaded fresh basil

1 cup grated pecorino Romano cheese

⅛ teaspoon salt

⅛ teaspoon freshly ground black pepper

1. Cook the pasta according to package directions.
2. In a medium sauté pan, heat the olive oil with the garlic over medium-high heat until the garlic begins to turn golden, about 1 minute. Immediately dump the garlic into a bowl large enough to handle all the ingredients.
3. Drain the pasta and add it to the bowl along with all the remaining ingredients. Toss well and serve immediately.

LORA'S LINGUINI WITH WHITE CLAM SAUCE

INGREDIENTS

Serves 2

½ pound linguini

2 tablespoons extra-virgin olive oil

½ small red onion, peeled and minced

3 cloves garlic, minced

1 tablespoon fresh thyme

Pinch red pepper flakes

½ cup dry white wine

1½ cups chicken broth

1 (10-ounce) can baby clams separated from the juice, juice reserved

2 tablespoons cornstarch dissolved in 2 tablespoons cold water

1 tablespoon butter

⅛ teaspoon salt

⅛ teaspoon freshly ground black pepper

1 cup grated Romano cheese

1. Bring a pot of water to a boil for the pasta. Boil the pasta according to package directions.

2. Meanwhile, heat the olive oil in a large saucepot over medium-high heat until barely smoking. Add the onion, garlic, thyme, and pepper flakes. Sauté about 3 minutes or until the onion begins to soften.

3. Add the wine and continue cooking until the volume is reduced by half.

4. Add the broth and the juice from the clams. Simmer gently about 7 minutes uncovered.

5. Slowly drizzle the cornstarch slurry into to the simmering sauce, constantly stirring the sauce. Remove from heat and add the clams and butter. Keep warm.

6. When the pasta is cooked, drain well and toss with the sauce. Season with salt and pepper. Divide the pasta between two serving plates and serve the cheese at the table to be sprinkled on top.

 PROPER PASTA ETIQUETTE

In Italy the pasta is almost always tossed with the sauce, not put in a bowl with the sauce ladled on top. Also, Italians do not use a spoon to load up a fork with pasta; they take smaller bites. It is not common to add cheese to fish-based sauces, but many do like cheese on this dish.

SPAGHETTI WITH MUSSELS AND PANCETTA

INGREDIENTS

Serves 2

½ pound spaghetti

2 tablespoons extra-virgin olive oil

2 ounces pancetta or bacon, small diced

3 cloves garlic, minced

Pinch red pepper flakes

1 cup dry white wine

1 (24-ounce) jar marinara sauce

1½ pounds fresh mussels, washed and debearded

⅛ teaspoon salt

⅛ teaspoon freshly ground black pepper

4 tablespoons chopped fresh parsley

1. Bring a pot of water to a boil for the pasta. Cook the pasta according to package directions.

2. In a large sauté pan, heat the oil over medium heat. Add the pancetta and cook until crispy, about 3–5 minutes. Transfer the pancetta to paper towels to drain and leave the fat in the pan.

3. Place the pan with the fat over medium-high heat and add the garlic and red pepper flakes. Sauté about 1 minute, then add the wine. Increase heat to high and cook until the wine is reduced by half.

4. Add the marinara and mussels. Keep the heat on high and cover the pot. Check the pot after about 3 minutes. The mussels are done when 95 percent of them have opened. Turn off the heat and remove and discard any unopened mussels. Keep sauce warm.

5. When the pasta is cooked, drain well and toss with the mussel sauce. Season with salt and pepper. Divide into two bowls. Top with parsley and serve.

 MUSSEL 101

Fresh mussels are available year-round. Many are farmed near Prince Edward Island and have the designation "PEI" mussels. Green-lipped mussels are from New Zealand, are much larger, and are always frozen. They are inferior in both flavor and texture. Always ask your fishmonger to tell you the date the mussels were harvested. By law, he or she must have this information.

PERCIATELLI WITH ARTICHOKES

INGREDIENTS

Serves 2

2 tablespoons extra-virgin
  olive oil

1 clove garlic, sliced

1 small red onion, peeled and
  minced

1 (8-ounce) can artichokes,
  drained

½ cup heavy cream

⅛ teaspoon salt

⅛ teaspoon freshly ground
  black pepper

½ pound perciatelli pasta

¼ cup grated Parmesan cheese

2 tablespoons chopped fresh dill

1. Heat the oil in a medium skillet over medium-high heat. Add the garlic and onion and sauté 3 minutes. Add the artichokes and cream and cook until the cream is reduced by half. Season with salt and pepper and keep warm.

2. Cook the pasta according to package directions. Drain the pasta and toss with the warm sauce. Top with the Parmesan and dill and serve.

RIGATONI WITH SIMPLE SHRIMP SCAMPI SAUCE

INGREDIENTS

Serves 2

½ pound rigatoni pasta

2 tablespoons extra-virgin
  olive oil

½ pound raw medium shrimp,
  shelled and deveined

4 cloves garlic, minced

1 teaspoon fresh thyme

½ cup dry white wine

1 cup clam juice

1 tablespoon butter

1. Bring a pot of water to a boil and cook the pasta according to package directions.

2. While the pasta is cooking, prepare the sauce. Over medium–high heat, heat the olive oil in a large skillet until barely smoking. Add the shrimp and brown quickly, about 2–3 minutes. Remove from the pan. The shrimp should be undercooked in the center.

3. Add the garlic and thyme to the pan, reduce heat to medium, and sauté 1 minute. Add the wine and reduce until almost evaporated.

4. Add the clam juice and cook until reduced by half. Add the shrimp, reduce to a simmer, and cook 2 minutes.

5. Turn off the heat and add the butter. Stir to melt, then toss the hot pasta with the sauce.

COLD PASTA WITH BUTTER BEANS AND TUNA

INGREDIENTS

Serves 2

—————

3 cups any cooked pasta, cooled

1 (15-ounce) can butter beans, drained and rinsed

1 (5-ounce) can good-quality tuna, drained and flaked

3 scallions, finely sliced

1 large ripe tomato, diced

2 tablespoons capers, rinsed

½ cup kalamata olives

Juice of ½ medium lemon

¼ cup extra-virgin olive oil

½ cup grated Parmesan cheese

⅛ teaspoon salt

⅛ teaspoon freshly ground black pepper

Mix all the ingredients together in a medium bowl and serve.

 TUNA 101
There are many kinds of canned tuna in the market these days. Look for albacore tuna that is "dolphin-safe." Solid tuna packed in water or olive oil works well for this dish. Tuna from Italy packed in extra-virgin olive oil is also a great choice for this dish. If using this type, do not drain the tuna, and cut back on the oil in the recipe.

JAPANESE-ITALIAN ANGEL HAIR PASTA

INGREDIENTS

Serves 2

—————

½ pound angel hair pasta

3 tablespoons extra-virgin olive oil

1 tablespoon butter

½ cup grated Parmesan cheese

½ cup tobiko (flying fish) caviar

10 shiso leaves, chiffonaded

⅛ teaspoon salt

⅛ teaspoon freshly ground black pepper

1. Cook the pasta in a medium stockpot until al dente according to package directions.
2. Drain the pasta and toss with the oil, butter, and cheese in a medium bowl.
3. When the butter is melted, add the caviar and shiso. Season with salt and pepper and toss to mix. Serve immediately.

 THE SIMILARITIES OF JAPAN AND ITALY
The common theme in Italian and Japanese cuisines is the respect for superior ingredients that are simply prepared. As an example, when sardines are in season, the Italians will prepare them by grilling them over wood and serving them with sea salt and lemon. In Japan they will also grill them, then sprinkle them with citrus-flavored soy sauce.

FARFALLE WITH CALAMARI FRA DIAVOLO SAUCE

INGREDIENTS

Serves 2

3 tablespoons extra-virgin olive oil

1 small red onion, peeled and finely diced

4 cloves garlic, minced

1 teaspoon red pepper flakes

¾ pound cleaned calamari, cut into rings and legs cut in half

1 cup dry red wine

1 (24-ounce) jar marinara sauce

1 cup clam juice

½ pound farfalle pasta

⅛ teaspoon salt

⅛ teaspoon freshly ground black pepper

1. In a medium saucepot, heat the oil over medium-high heat until barley smoking. Add the onion, garlic, and red pepper flakes. Sauté about 3 minutes or until the onion begins to soften.
2. Add the calamari and red wine. Increase the heat to high and reduce the wine until almost evaporated.
3. Add the marinara and clam juice. Reduce heat and simmer very gently 2 hours covered.
4. When the sauce is nearly finished, cook the pasta according to package directions. Season the sauce with salt and pepper, toss with the drained pasta, and serve.

 CALAMARI 101

Calamari is the Italian word for "squid." There are many species and sizes of squid in the sea, but what we commonly see in the fish market are small squid about 6"–10" long. Most cleaned squid have previously been frozen. Fresh squid are superior in flavor but are difficult and messy to clean.

ISRAELI COUSCOUS "RISOTTO" PRIMAVERA

INGREDIENTS

Serves 2

1 quart chicken or vegetable broth

4 tablespoons extra-virgin olive oil, divided

½ pound Israeli couscous

1 small white onion, peeled and finely diced

1 small red bell pepper, seeded and finely diced

1 small zucchini, finely diced

½ cup asparagus tips

2 cloves garlic, minced

½ cup grated Parmesan cheese

2 tablespoons finely minced fresh chives

⅛ teaspoon salt

⅛ teaspoon freshly ground black pepper

1. In a medium saucepan, heat the broth over medium heat until almost boiling.
2. Meanwhile, in a small sauté pan, heat half of the oil over medium heat. Add the couscous and toss well in the oil. Cook until golden, about 5 minutes, stirring often. Remove the couscous from the pan and set aside.
3. In the same pan, heat the remaining oil until barely smoking. Add the onion, bell pepper, zucchini, asparagus, and garlic. Sauté about 3 minutes.
4. Return the couscous to the pan with the vegetables and add about one-third of the hot broth. Cook uncovered over low heat until the broth has been absorbed, stirring occasionally. Repeat the process, adding more broth in portions until the couscous is al dente and almost all of the broth has been absorbed.
5. Turn off heat and add the Parmesan cheese and chives. Season with salt and pepper and serve.

THE RISOTTO METHOD

Usually associated with the classic Italian rice dish, adding hot broth gradually to short-grained starchy rice results in a creamy texture that is prized in a good risotto. This couscous is unique and acts much in the same way.

CAVATELLI WITH WHITE BEANS AND ARUGULA

INGREDIENTS

Serves 2

---

4 tablespoons extra-virgin olive oil

2 cloves garlic, sliced

½ pound cavatelli pasta

1 (15.5-ounce) can small white beans, drained and rinsed

2 cups washed arugula leaves

½ cup shaved Parmesan cheese

⅛ teaspoon salt

⅛ teaspoon freshly ground black pepper

1. In a medium skillet, heat the olive oil over medium-high heat; add the garlic and cook until it turns golden, about 1 minute. Immediately remove from heat.

2. Cook the pasta according to package directions. Drain the pasta and place in a large bowl. Add the garlic and oil and remaining ingredients to the bowl and mix together. The arugula will wilt and collapse. Serve immediately.

 THE SIMPLEST SAUCE

The combination of Parmesan cheese and olive oil transforms plain pasta into a real treat. This combination, with the addition of any number of pantry ingredients, can create countless pasta masterpieces.

SPAGHETTI WITH "SAND"

INGREDIENTS

Serves 2

½ pound thin spaghetti

¼ cup extra-virgin olive oil

1 tablespoon butter

½ cup plain bread crumbs

1 clove garlic, minced

¼ cup grated Parmesan cheese

¼ cup chopped fresh parsley

⅛ teaspoon salt

⅛ teaspoon freshly ground black pepper

1. Bring a pot of water to a boil and cook the pasta according to package directions.

2. While the pasta is cooking, heat the olive oil and butter together in a medium skillet over medium-high heat until the butter stops bubbling.

3. Add the bread crumbs and the garlic. Toast the bread crumbs over medium heat about 4 minutes, stirring frequently. (Be careful not to burn the bread crumbs.)

4. Drain the pasta, toss with the bread crumb mixture, and then toss with the cheese and parsley. Season with salt and pepper and serve.

 CRUMMY BUSINESS

Bread crumbs are a simple and effective way to add texture to a variety of dishes. Toasted bread crumbs are great on top of boiled veggies. They can also be used as a simple thickener for sauces and soups.

WILD RICE VEGETABLE PANCAKES

INGREDIENTS

Serves 2

⅓ cup wild rice

1 cup lightly salted water

⅓ cup julienned carrots

⅓ cup julienned celery

⅓ cup julienned white onion

1 scallion, chopped

1 large egg

3 tablespoons all-purpose flour

¼ teaspoon kosher salt

⅛ teaspoon freshly ground
   black pepper

2 tablespoons extra-virgin
   olive oil

1. Add the wild rice and 1 cup lightly salted water to a small saucepan and boil until very tender and most grains have burst open, about 40 minutes. Drain, reserving liquid, and cool the rice by spreading it on a platter or pan.

2. In a large bowl, toss the rice with the carrots, celery, onion, scallions, egg, and flour. Season with salt and pepper. Moisten with a few drops of rice-cooking liquid to help the mixture adhere to itself.

3. Heat olive oil in a medium nonstick skillet over medium heat until a piece of onion sizzles when added, about 2 minutes. Place ¼-cup mounds of rice mixture into the pan; shape them into rough-hewn pancakes. Cook without moving them until they brown on the first side and are visibly cooked around the edges, about 5 minutes.

4. Flip the pancakes with a spatula and cook until lightly browned on the second side, about 3–4 minutes. Drain and serve.

SPINACH NOODLES WITH SMOKED HAM

INGREDIENTS

Serves 2

2 tablespoons extra-virgin
   olive oil

1 cup sliced mushrooms

½ cup julienned smoked ham

1 cup fresh peas

½ cup heavy cream

⅛ teaspoon salt

⅛ teaspoon freshly ground
   black pepper

½ pound spinach fettuccini

¼ cup grated Parmesan cheese

1. Heat the olive oil in a medium skillet over medium-high heat. Add the mushrooms. Sauté about 3 minutes or until they just begin to soften. Add the ham and peas and sauté 3 more minutes.

2. Add the cream and cook until it is reduced by half. Season with salt and pepper.

3. Meanwhile, cook the pasta according to package directions. Drain and toss with the warm sauce. Place in two bowls, top each bowl with the Parmesan, and serve.

GARGANELLI WITH PORCINI AND TOMATO SAUCE

INGREDIENTS

Serves 2

1 cup dried porcini mushrooms

2 cups warm water

3 tablespoons extra-virgin olive oil

1 small white onion, peeled and small diced

Pinch red pepper flakes

½ cup dry red wine

1 (24-ounce) jar marinara sauce

⅛ teaspoon salt

⅛ teaspoon freshly ground black pepper

½ pound garganelli pasta

½ cup grated Parmesan cheese

¼ cup chopped fresh parsley

1. In a medium bowl, soak the porcini mushrooms in the warm water 1 hour. Remove the mushrooms from the water and roughly chop them. Strain the soaking liquid to remove any sand. Reserve 1 cup of the liquid.

2. Heat the olive oil over medium-high heat in a medium saucepot. Add the onion and red pepper flakes and sauté 3 minutes or until the onion begins to soften. Add the wine and reduce by half.

3. Add the mushrooms, the mushroom soaking water, and the marinara. Simmer gently over low heat 1 hour uncovered. Season with salt and pepper and keep warm.

4. Cook the pasta according to the package directions, drain, and toss with the warm sauce. Serve with the cheese and parsley sprinkled over the top.

 THE KING

Porcini literally translates to "little pig" in Italian. These mushrooms are the most sought-after wild mushroom on earth. The Latin *Boletus edulis* is the scientific name for these earthy delights. Some mushroom foragers in the Pacific Northwest of the United States have been killed for encroaching on other mushroom foragers' turf.

CHAPTER 13

Desserts

PEARS POACHED IN WHITE WINE AND VANILLA

INGREDIENTS

Serves 2

2 cups water

2 cups dry white wine

Juice of 1 medium lemon

2 medium firm pears, peeled and cored

1 cinnamon stick

2 cups granulated sugar

1 vanilla bean, split

1. In a medium pot, mix together the water, wine, and lemon juice. Add the pears, cinnamon, sugar, and vanilla and heat over medium heat to just below a simmer.
2. Place a clean dish towel on top of the pears to keep them from floating too high. Allow the towel to totally soak.
3. Cook on a gentle simmer 13 minutes or until a small knife inserted in the bottom of the pear comes free with no resistance. Pour the pears and liquid into a shallow dish and place in the refrigerator to cool uncovered, around 1 hour. Serve the pears in bowls with some of the liquid poured on top.

POACHING VERSUS BOILING

The difference between boiling and poaching is the temperature and movement of the water. Poach items that are delicate and risk falling apart if cooked too fast, such as fruit or fish. The temperature of the liquid should be between 185°F and 200°F so the water does not move fast or boil.

PINEAPPLE WITH CARAMEL ICE CREAM

INGREDIENTS

Serves 2

½ medium pineapple, peeled, cored, and cut into ½"-thick slices

2 tablespoons vegetable oil

⅛ teaspoon salt

⅛ teaspoon freshly ground black pepper

3 cups caramel (or dulce de leche) ice cream

1. In a medium bowl, toss the pineapple with the oil, salt, and pepper. Add to a medium nonstick skillet and sauté over high heat until both sides are well browned, about 8 minutes. Place on a cutting board and chop into bite-sized pieces.
2. Place the ice cream in bowls and top with the warm pineapple chunks.

SALT AND PEPPER ON DESSERT?

Most desserts have a salt component because salt helps the human palate to better recognize different tastes. The desserts are not "salty" but just plain taste better. Adding pepper to this and other desserts brings an interesting note that is hard to pinpoint, but creates a level of complexity and surprise.

STRAWBERRIES WITH BALSAMIC SYRUP

INGREDIENTS

Serves 2

1 cup balsamic vinegar

¼ cup granulated sugar

1 quart fresh strawberries, sliced

In a small saucepan over medium-low heat, combine the vinegar and sugar and simmer until about ⅓ of a cup remains. Let cool to room temperature. Drizzle all over the berries and enjoy.

CHOCOLATE RASPBERRY PIE

INGREDIENTS

Yields 1 pie

1 cup semisweet chocolate chips

1 (8-ounce) package cream cheese, softened

1 (9") chocolate cookie pie crust

¼ cup raspberry jelly

2 cups fresh raspberries

1. Add the chocolate chips to the top of a double boiler over simmering water and heat until melted smooth and warm, stirring occasionally. Remove from heat.
2. Cut cream cheese into cubes and add to melted chips; beat well until smooth. Place mixture in refrigerator 10 minutes.
3. Spread cooled chocolate mixture in bottom of pie crust.
4. Put jelly in a medium saucepan over low heat; cook and stir just until jelly is almost melted. Remove from heat and gently fold in raspberries just until coated. Place on top of the chocolate mixture. Serve immediately or cover and refrigerate until serving time.

STRAWBERRIES WITH SOUR CREAM

INGREDIENTS

Serves 2

1 pint strawberries, stemmed and sliced

½ cup sour cream

¼ cup brown sugar

⅛ cup toasted pecans

In a glass serving bowl, place one-third of the strawberries. Top with one-third of the sour cream, and sprinkle with one-third of the brown sugar. Repeat layers, ending with brown sugar. Top with toasted pecans and serve or cover and refrigerate up to 8 hours.

CHOCO-PEANUT CRUNCHERS

INGREDIENTS
Yields 12 candies

¾ cup semisweet chocolate chips

1 tablespoon plus 2 teaspoons peanut butter

⅓ cup raw unsalted cashews

⅓ cup miniature marshmallows

⅓ cup crisp rice cereal

1. Line a cookie sheet with parchment paper or waxed paper and set aside.
2. Add the chocolate chips and peanut butter to the top of a double boiler over simmering water and heat until melted smooth and warm, stirring occasionally. Remove from heat.
3. Stir in remaining ingredients until coated. Drop mixture by spoonfuls onto prepared cookie sheet and refrigerate until set. Store in an airtight container at room temperature.

 ABOUT SEMISWEET CHOCOLATE
Semisweet chocolate is made of cocoa butter (made from roasted, ground cocoa bean nibs), sugar, and vanilla. Semisweet chocolate chips are generally a bit sweeter than bar chocolate. You can substitute one for the other. Chop semisweet chocolate bars into small pieces to use in place of the chips if you prefer.

EASY FUDGE

INGREDIENTS
Serves 2

¾ cup semisweet chocolate chips

3 tablespoons milk chocolate chips

½ cup sweetened condensed milk

½ cup chopped unsalted cashews

½ cup miniature marshmallows

1. Grease a small square glass pan with butter and set aside.
2. Add the semisweet chocolate chips, milk chocolate chips, and sweetened condensed milk to the top of a double boiler over simmering water and heat until melted smooth and warm, stirring occasionally. Remove from heat.
3. Stir in cashews until mixed, then stir in marshmallows. Spread into prepared pan and let stand until cool.

 SWEETENED CONDENSED MILK
Sweetened condensed milk was invented in the 1800s to prevent food poisoning in infants and children that was caused by lack of pasteurization and refrigeration. It's a combination of milk and sugar with 50 percent of the water removed. Keep a can or two on hand because it's a great ingredient for making fudge and candies.

DARK CHOCOLATE "SALAMI" WITH BISCOTTI CHUNKS

INGREDIENTS

Serves 2

7 ounces sweetened condensed milk

10 ounces semisweet chocolate chips

1 tablespoon butter

½ cup chopped toasted hazelnuts

2 biscotti cookies, broken into ¼" pieces

1. In a small saucepan, heat the condensed milk, chocolate, and butter over low heat until smooth. Remove from heat and add the hazelnuts and biscotti pieces.
2. Pour out onto a cookie sheet lined with plastic wrap and let cool 10 minutes.
3. Roll the plastic wrap around the mixture and form into a long tube. Tighten the ends down and refrigerate until firm. Unwrap, slice, and serve.

 SWEETNESS IN CHOCOLATE

Chocolate has many levels of sweetness. Milk, semisweet, bitter, and unsweetened are just a few. The recipe here can be made with any kind of chocolate, but semisweet is recommended because the milk is so sweet. Americans tend to like milk chocolate, while Europeans prefer more bitter chocolates. Experiment and see which type you like the best.

CEREAL CARAMEL CHEWS

INGREDIENTS
Yields 12 bars

Butter, as needed
½ cup corn syrup
½ cup brown sugar
1 cup crunchy peanut butter
3 cups cornflakes
1 cup milk chocolate chips

1. Grease a 9" × 13" pan with butter and set aside.
2. In a medium saucepan, combine corn syrup and brown sugar. Cook over medium heat until mixture boils, stirring frequently. Let boil 2 minutes, stirring constantly.
3. Remove from heat and add peanut butter; stir until melted. Add cornflakes and stir gently, then spread into prepared pan. Press down with the back of a greased spoon to form an even surface.
4. Add the chocolate chips to the top of a double boiler over simmering water and heat until melted smooth and warm, stirring occasionally. Remove from heat. Pour over cereal mixture and spread; let cool. Cut into bars.

CHOCOLATE DATE BALLS

INGREDIENTS
Yields 12 balls

¼ cup unsalted butter
¼ cup granulated sugar
2 tablespoons brown sugar
½ cup finely chopped dates
1 large egg, beaten
½ cup semisweet chocolate chips
¼ teaspoon vanilla
1 cup crisp rice cereal
¼ cup powdered sugar

1. In a medium saucepan, melt butter, sugar, and brown sugar together over medium heat. Stir in dates and bring to a boil. Cook mixture, stirring constantly, 3–4 minutes until dates begin to melt. Add egg and cook 1 minute longer, stirring constantly.
2. Add chocolate chips, remove pan from heat, cover, and let stand 4–5 minutes. Add vanilla and stir until chocolate melts and mixture is blended.
3. Add rice cereal to date mixture. Spread powdered sugar onto a shallow plate. Drop date mixture by the heaping tablespoonful into powdered sugar and form into balls. Place on cookie sheet; let stand until cool and firm.

 ABOUT DATES
You can buy dates in the baking aisle of the supermarket, and sometimes in the produce department. When choosing dates for baking and cooking, do not use the dates that are precut and rolled in sugar. They are often too dry and do not blend well in cookie dough.

CARAMEL APPLE PARFAITS

INGREDIENTS

Serves 2

2 tablespoons granulated sugar

¼ teaspoon ground cinnamon

1 small Granny Smith apple, peeled and chopped

2 tablespoons unsalted butter

1 cup vanilla ice cream

2 shortbread cookies, crumbled

2 tablespoons chopped toasted pecans

1. In a medium bowl, combine sugar, cinnamon, and apples and toss to coat.
2. Melt butter in a medium saucepan and add apple mixture. Cook over low heat 10–12 minutes or until apples are tender and sauce is lightly caramelized. Remove from heat, pour mixture into a heatproof bowl, and let stand 10 minutes, stirring occasionally.
3. Make parfaits by layering apple mixture, ice cream, crumbled shortbread cookies, and pecans in individual glasses. Serve immediately.

 COOKING APPLES

There are apples that are best for eating out of hand, and those best for cooking. Cooking apples include McIntosh, Cortland, Rome Beauty, Jonathan, Haralson, and Granny Smith. The best apples for eating out of hand include Honeycrisp, Gala, Red Delicious, and new varieties including Sweet Sixteen and Honeygold.

NO-BAKE APPLE COOKIES

INGREDIENTS

Yields 12 cookies

2 tablespoons unsalted butter

6 tablespoons granulated sugar

2 tablespoons brown sugar

¼ cup peeled and grated Granny Smith apple

⅛ teaspoon ground cinnamon

¾ cup quick-cooking oatmeal

¼ cup chopped walnuts

2 tablespoons powdered sugar

1. In a medium saucepan, melt butter with granulated and brown sugars over medium heat; stir in apple. Bring to a boil and stir 1–2 minutes until well combined and bubbling. Remove from heat and add cinnamon, oatmeal, and walnuts; stir to combine. Let stand 10 minutes.
2. Spread powdered sugar onto a shallow plate. Carefully drop apple mixture by the teaspoonful into powdered sugar and roll into balls. Place on waxed paper and let stand until the cookies are firm.

US/METRIC CONVERSION CHART

VOLUME CONVERSIONS

US Volume Measure	Metric Equivalent
⅛ teaspoon	0.5 milliliter
¼ teaspoon	1 milliliter
½ teaspoon	2 milliliters
1 teaspoon	5 milliliters
½ tablespoon	7 milliliters
1 tablespoon (3 teaspoons)	15 milliliters
2 tablespoons (1 fluid ounce)	30 milliliters
¼ cup (4 tablespoons)	60 milliliters
⅓ cup	90 milliliters
½ cup (4 fluid ounces)	125 milliliters
⅔ cup	160 milliliters
¾ cup (6 fluid ounces)	180 milliliters
1 cup (16 tablespoons)	250 milliliters
1 pint (2 cups)	500 milliliters
1 quart (4 cups)	1 liter (about)

WEIGHT CONVERSIONS

US Weight Measure	Metric Equivalent
½ ounce	15 grams
1 ounce	30 grams
2 ounces	60 grams
3 ounces	85 grams
¼ pound (4 ounces)	115 grams
½ pound (8 ounces)	225 grams
¾ pound (12 ounces)	340 grams
1 pound (16 ounces)	454 grams

OVEN TEMPERATURE CONVERSIONS

Degrees Fahrenheit	Degrees Celsius
200 degrees F	95 degrees C
250 degrees F	120 degrees C
275 degrees F	135 degrees C
300 degrees F	150 degrees C
325 degrees F	160 degrees C
350 degrees F	180 degrees C
375 degrees F	190 degrees C
400 degrees F	205 degrees C
425 degrees F	220 degrees C
450 degrees F	230 degrees C

BAKING PAN SIZES

American	Metric
8 x 1½ inch round baking pan	20 x 4 cm cake tin
9 x 1½ inch round baking pan	23 x 3.5 cm cake tin
11 x 7 x 1½ inch baking pan	28 x 18 x 4 cm baking tin
13 x 9 x 2 inch baking pan	30 x 20 x 5 cm baking tin
2 quart rectangular baking dish	30 x 20 x 3 cm baking tin
15 x 10 x 2 inch baking pan	30 x 25 x 2 cm baking tin (Swiss roll tin)
9 inch pie plate	22 x 4 or 23 x 4 cm pie plate
7 or 8 inch springform pan	18 or 20 cm springform or loose bottom cake tin
9 x 5 x 3 inch loaf pan	23 x 13 x 7 cm or 2 lb narrow loaf or pate tin
1½ quart casserole	1.5 liter casserole
2 quart casserole	2 liter casserole

INDEX